# The Salt Factor

influence your environment with the values and character of Christ

Sino Agueze

AuthorHouse™
1663 Liberty Drive
Bloomington, IN 47403
www.authorhouse.com
Phone: 1-800-839-8640

© 2010 Sino Agueze. All rights reserved.

No part of this book may be reproduced, stored in a retrieval system, or transmitted by any means without the written permission of the author.

First published by AuthorHouse  3/15/2010

ISBN: 978-1-4490-8053-2 (e)
ISBN: 978-1-4490-8051-8 (sc)
ISBN: 978-1-4490-8052-5 (hc)

Library of Congress Control Number: 2010902021

Printed in the United States of America
Bloomington, Indiana

This book is printed on acid-free paper.

Unless otherwise indicated, all Scripture quotations are
taken from the King James Version of the Bible.

"Scripture taken from the New King James Version. Copyright © 1982 by Thomas Nelson,   Inc. Used by permission. All rights reserved."

Scripture quotations marked NLT are taken from the Holy Bible, New Living Translation, copyright 1996, 2004. Used by permission of Tyndale House Publishers, Inc., Wheaton, Illinois 60189. All rights reserved.

Scripture taken from The Message. Copyright © 1993, 1994, 1995, 1996, 2000, 2001, 2002. Used by permission of NavPress Publishing Group."

"Scripture quotations taken from the Amplified® Bible,
Copyright © 1954, 1958, 1962, 1964, 1965, 1987 by The Lockman Foundation
Used by permission." (www.Lockman.org)

Copyright 1998 by David H. Stern. Published by Jewish New Testament Publications, Inc. All rights reserved. Used by permission.

"Scripture quotations are from The Holy Bible, English Standard Version® (ESV®), copyright © 2001 by Crossway, a publishing ministry of Good News Publishers. Used by permission. All rights reserved."

# DEDICATION

i dedicate this book to five groups of people…

I
all those who seek to be agents of change in
enhancing the value of life on earth

II
those who long to understand the role systems and
structures play in determining the destiny of nations

III
those humble enough to re-examine the
mandate of the great commission

IV
all those who desire to live a remarkable and meaningful life

V
those who want to live by nothing less than
the standard of life lived by jesus christ.

# ACKNOWLEDGEMENTS

I must first acknowledge the Lord Jesus Christ for giving me the passion to write and publish this book. It was His urgency and emotion I felt compelling me to get this book out to the nations.

To Dr. Sunday Adelaja, a true mentor and friend, thank you for inspiring me in so many ways, and for modeling before me the authentic life of Christ in your life, home and ministry.

I want to thank Christopher Baldwin, President of DustVISION, for designing the cover of this book as well as his contributions during the writing process. I also must acknowledge Lucretia Williams, for her tireless effort in seeing this project through completion.

Finally, I want to thank my one and only wife, Janette, for all of her work revising and editing this book. I deeply appreciate you pouring your very heart and soul into this work, all for the cause of Christ. I love you dearly.

# CONTENTS

**FOREWORD** ............................................. xi

**INTRODUCTION** ........................................ xiii

**CHAPTER 1: SALT IN A SALT SHAKER** ..................... 1
"SAVIORS IN ZION"

**CHAPTER 2: HOW SALT WORKS IN A SOUP** ................. 15
"KINGDOM PRINCIPLES FOR TRANSFORMING WORLD-SYSTEMS"

**CHAPTER 3: THE TWO MAIN FUNCTIONS OF SALT** ........... 41
"KINGDOM RESPONSIBILITIES OF A BELIEVER"

**CHAPTER 4: HINDRANCES TO A SALTED LIFE** .............. 74
"KINGDOM CHARACTER AND KINGDOM VALUES"

**CHAPTER 5: SEASONING THE WORLD WITH LOVE** ........... 119
"THE NATURE OF THE KING AND HIS KINGDOM"

**CHAPTER 6: THE ESSENCE OF THE SALT LIFE** ............ 139
"KINGDOM KEYS TO THE DISCIPLESHIP OF NATIONS"

**CONCLUSION** ........................................ 148

# FOREWORD

Every great teacher dreams of inspiring a follower who will be able to take his masterpiece and improve on it. Pastor Sino Agueze is such one whose potential for greatness exudes from within his very core. I am blessed to call him my friend and my brother.

This book is a product of my relationship with Pastor Sino, and his desire, not just to change, but also to be a change agent. The world would be a better place if there were more pastors willing to pay the price for change, like Pastor Sino.

If you really wish to know the purpose of the church, her mission and calling, then this book is a must read for you. Every believer that wishes to discover themselves in this kingdom will find this book exciting. The message within its pages is life transforming and will never leave you where it finds you. Without a doubt, you will be taken to a higher level in Christ Jesus by coming in touch with this book.

May the Lord honor the revelation of this book and use it as a catalyst to building a better world through each of you.

God bless you!

With Love,

Pastor Sunday Adelaja
Embassy of God
Kiev, Ukraine

# INTRODUCTION

This book has an amazing story behind it. I had the privilege of accompanying Pastor Sunday Adelaja, of the Embassy of God Church in Ukraine, to Japan in September of 2008. He was invited to address one of the largest Christian gatherings in the history of Japan. It was at this meeting that He taught on the message: "Ye are the Salt of the Earth." The message was simple but life transforming. On our way back from the meeting, I expressed how big of an impact the message had on me. I experienced a strong leading to develop the message even further into a book. The excitement on Dr. Sunday's face was apparent, as he encouraged me to take hold of this dream and make it a reality. I will always remain grateful to him for helping me to understand the concept of the Kingdom in its purest form. This book is truly a result of my relationship with him and I am deeply grateful God has placed him in my life.

The reason I am excited about this book is not because I wrote it, but because my heart and soul went into every word written within its pages. It was important to me that this work be relevant and more than just another book on the shelf. My heart's desire is that those who read it be dramatically transformed by its message. God's presence has been prayed into every page with the hope that it will enlighten, inspire and mobilize the transformed heart to change the world with the character of Christ the King, and the values of His kingdom.

The message in this book will revolutionize your life and give you a new understanding of the Great Commission. You will understand what Jesus meant when He instructed us to go into the world and make disciples of all nations. There is only one way to win the world for Christ in the 21st century, and it will be unveiled in these chapters as you become familiar with, and understand, the discipleship of nations.

It is my sincere prayer that your life be forever transformed by the revelation received from reading this book, and that the world will become a better place through you applying the principles within its pages. May you discover the true purpose of the church, and in doing so, the true purpose of your own life.

Sino Agueze

# Chapter 1
# SALT IN A SALT SHAKER
## "SAVIORS IN ZION"

*"Pastors are the wardens; and their members are the prisoners." – Dr. Sunday Adelaja*

It is time to re-define the reason why the body of Christ exists on planet earth. God's intent for establishing the church must not only be understood, but her purpose must be clearly defined in order to appreciate her value and her responsibility in discipling nations, and restoring the earth back to God. The church, as the body of Christ, is the only living, active presence of Jesus Christ in the earth. Without her, God has no voice, no presence and no authority in the world around us. This is why the church must regain her God-given influence and become a meaningful force in the earth.

> *"Who is left among you that saw this house in her first glory? and how do ye see it now? is it not in your eyes in comparison of it as nothing?" (Haggai 2:3 KJV)*

The church is God's visible presence in the world and the only means of mirroring the visibility of God to people in the world. Every Christian should desire to see the church restored to her original glory, to see Christ glorified, lifted up and represented well. Each and every believer has gifts, talents and abilities that are placed inside of them in order to fulfill God's assignment for their life, and ultimately, His kingdom.

The entire world is waiting for God's children to rise up and become saviors and deliverers in the earth (Romans 8:19-22). Christians have been commissioned to deliver mankind and release them from suffering. Everyone living without God is suffering, and only the children of God possess the power that can destroy evil in the world. As long as people remain in bondage to sin and futility, their sorrow and suffering will remain. There are people waiting to be delivered, waiting to be set free from the humiliation and shame of sin. Whether people recognize it or not, everyone is trying to find God, and everyone needs God and His life-giving power. This is where Christians come in. No one has ever seen God, but the body of Christ, the church, is His visible presence in the earth. Even as Jesus came to reveal the Father, believers are to reveal Christ to a world that desperately needs Him. People need the freedom that comes from God, true spiritual freedom, and as citizens of the Kingdom of God, ambassadors for Christ, believers are the saviors to the world. Now is the time to become jealous for Zion and the glory of her King, and to finish the assignment that Jesus Christ has given to the church.

> *"That he might present it to himself a glorious church, not having spot, or wrinkle, or any such thing; but that it should be holy and without blemish." (Ephesians 5:27 KJV)*

> *"The king's daughter is all glorious within: her clothing is of wrought gold." (Psalms 45:13 KJV)*

Too many Christians have been locked up within the four walls of the church and limited in their ability to become true saviors in the world today. The church of Jesus Christ is not meant to be a place where people attend, render service or financial assistance and then go back to their own lives. The church today has become an amoeba church. An amoeba is a one celled organism that lives for itself; it does not have the capacity to reproduce. They are shapeless and formless, and this explains why the church is not the pillar she was designed to be. The church has become one dimensional, and withdrawn herself from the world she was intended to penetrate. The church is currently the least influential organization, because it abides alone, when she was designed to be the greatest.

This is not the picture or blueprint of the church that was left by Jesus Christ. God is building a glorious church. This glory starts from within and shines out with the sole intent of revealing who the Savior really is. This church is to be living and vibrant, full of beauty and purity, full of power and authority, with a heart to serve humanity. She is made up of men and women, of all ages and ethnicities, who carry the mandate of revealing Christ to the world by taking on His character and values and living them out in everyday life as the salt of the earth.

## THE GLORY AND INFLUENCE OF THE CHURCH

*"And it shall come to pass in the last days, that the mountain of the LORD'S house shall be established in the top of the mountains, and shall be exalted above the hills; and all nations shall flow unto it. And many people shall go and say, Come ye, and let us go up to the mountain of the LORD, to the house of the God of Jacob; and he will teach us of his ways, and we will walk in his paths: for out of Zion shall go forth the law, and the word of the LORD from Jerusalem." (Isaiah 2:2-3 KJV)*

The above passage is a clear blueprint of God's intent for His church. Here the church is compared to a mountain that is established above all other mountains, which means that nothing in this world should compare to the influence of the church. Her influence is to exceed far beyond any other institution or organization in the world. Mountains and hills represent these institutions, but the church is designed to exceed them all in glory. She is to be a shining light to all the nations of the earth, a city set on a hill for all to see. Her influence is to be known and felt throughout the four corners of the earth.

If this is the intent and plan of God, why is this not the present condition of the church? Why are other organizations seemingly more reputable and relied upon by the world? God has not been unfaithful in doing His part; it is because the church has not captured the deeper meaning of the Great Commission, which is, that saviors and deliverers are to be raised as the salt of the earth, in the church, and released into the world to preserve society from decay. This is the only way not to be trampled under the feet of men. The church's impact in transforming people and culture should be second to none. Zion, in the scriptures, speaks of the church, and she will once again regain her God-given responsibility of teaching nations the principles of God's kingdom, which will cause them to be primarily concerned with walking in His ways.

> *"And many people shall go and say, Come ye, and let us go up to the mountain of the LORD, to the house of the God of Jacob; and he will teach us of his ways, and we will walk in his paths." (Isaiah 2:3 KJV)*

As the light of the world, the church will radiate God's glory and the nations of the earth will be drawn to her light. The brighter her light shines, and the more influence she carries, the nations of the world will be attracted to her and the values she represents. The beauty of Christ will be the force behind her influence, and as the sun lightens the day, so shall the church lighten the earth with the glory of her King.

> *"Beautiful for situation, the joy of the whole earth, is Mount Zion, on the sides of the north, the city of the great King. Walk about Zion, and go round about her: tell the towers thereof. Mark ye well her bulwarks, consider her palaces; that ye may tell it to the generation following." (Psalms 48: 2, 12-13 KJV)*

In God's eyes, the church is the joy of the whole earth. Isn't this an amazing thought? That the church has the capacity to bring joy and satisfaction to every heart? God has elevated and beautifully positioned her for the entire world to see. She is not insignificant, nor is she invisible. In fact, the church is so valuable that the world can't exist or survive without her. Her towers, bulwarks and palaces represent her structures, principles and value-systems; they are worth emulating. They are superior to the failing systems of this world. The world should learn from the church, rather than her adapting to the trends of the world. No other organization or institution has the capacity to produce her works or to deeply transform the lives of people. Only those who are born of God, those who possess His "DNA" as His children, can inherit His characteristics. The church of the Lord Jesus Christ is the only hope for the world.

## THE STRENGTH AND DOMINION OF THE CHURCH

*"The LORD shall send the rod of thy strength out of Zion: rule thou in the midst of thine enemies." (Psalms 110:2 KJV)*

The Lord will rule over the kingdoms and systems of this world through His body - the church. All enemies to the cross of Christ will be subdued, and it is through God's people that the power of God will be revealed like never before. *"To the intent that now unto the principalities and powers in heavenly places might be known by the church the manifold wisdom of God"* (Ephesians 3:10 KJV). There is going to be a display of the wisdom of God manifesting in a tangible form that is far superior to the wisdom of this world. This wisdom will manifest in superior sciences, solving global crisis, and this key is in the hands of the church. No force in this world will match that of the church, and the preeminence of Christ will be visible in all spheres of society.

*"They go from strength to strength; every one of them in Zion appeareth before God." (Psalms 84:7 KJV)*

The power of heaven will drive the operations of the church, as Christ Himself stands behind the church as her very source of strength.

She will always experience an upward and forward movement. Her momentum will be unstoppable and she will triumph victoriously over the world's system. With God's ability at work in Zion, nothing will be able to stand in her way of achieving her glorious destiny, which is raising saviors that carry the kingdom culture of Jesus Christ.

## THE BEAUTY AND EXCELLENCE OF THE CHURCH

> *"Glorious things are spoken of thee, O city of God. Selah." (Psalms 87:3 KJV)*

There is a beauty and excellence that will accompany the church and her fame will reach all corners of the earth. Her exploits will be known throughout the nations and they will know of her God. This beauty and excellence will exalt her King and show that the God in the midst of her is mighty. The nations of the world will speak her praise and publish her works throughout the earth. The church's influence will astonish the minds of men and shut the mouth of the prideful. Then her glory will be restored and the Lord will reign through her.

> *"And of Zion it shall be said, this and that man was born in her: and the highest himself shall establish her." (Psalms 87:5 KJV)*

Everyone who is born in her will be distinguished with excellence. They will dwell in a class of their own and function as true ambassadors of the kingdom of God. They will be distinct in every way, for they are born of God. Christians will be known by their results and proofs and they will be known as a people who are not of this world.

> *"The mighty God, even the LORD, hath spoken, and called the earth from the rising of the sun unto the going down thereof. Out of Zion, the perfection of beauty, God hath shined." (Psalms 50:1-2 KJV)*

God is calling the earth back to Himself through the church. When the world sees the beauty of Zion, they will see the true beauty of God. What makes the church beautiful is what also made Christ beautiful. His values and virtues will reveal the emptiness and futility of the world and draw them to Himself. This is why believers must be clothed with the beauty of His life, character and love if they are to remain relevant and not lose their saltiness in the world. Nothing is as beautiful as Christ, so children of God must engulf themselves in Him. They must put on Christ Jesus. *"For as many of you as have been baptized into Christ have put on Christ" (Gal 3:27 KJV).* The world must see Jesus living and flowing through His followers. The objective of all church activities should be centered on Christ and the cause of His kingdom, which is to have Christ revealed to us, in us and ultimately through us.

## WHY THE CHURCH EXISTS

> *"And he gave some, apostles; and some, prophets; and some, evangelists; and some, pastors and teachers; For the perfecting of the saints, for the work of the ministry, for the edifying of the body of Christ: Till we all come in the unity of the faith, and of the knowledge of the Son of God, unto a perfect man, unto the measure of the stature of the fullness of Christ..." (Ephesians 4:11-13 KJV)*

The church can easily be compared to a training center, a place where Christians are taught and developed into the likeness of Jesus Christ. The primary responsibility of every local church is to raise saviors who can impact and transform their environment with the character of King and the values of His kingdom. These are people who can take what they have learned and apply it and live it out in their daily lives. The mindset the church should carry is that Sundays are for training, and ministry is what she does Monday through Saturday.

> *"And saviors shall come up on mount Zion to judge the mount of Esau; and the kingdom shall be the Lord's."*
> *(Obadiah 1:21 KJV)*

The maturity of believers is a means to an end, and not an end in itself. Maturity is what provides a platform for Christians to transform the world. As they become more like Christ, possess His character and values, they are able to live beyond themselves and bring change to their environment. Only those who have "put on Christ" can give the world a true visibility of the life of God.

Listed below are some erroneous concepts that exist in regards to the church. Now please understand that they are not all wrong, or bad, but these mindsets do not capture the full picture of the church's purpose. Each one, when viewed separately, does not provide an accurate view of the body of Christ, and as a result, the church is not in a position to fulfill the mandate of the Great Commission that she will be held accountable for.

## ERRONEOUS CONCEPTS

- Some think the church exists simply to increase membership
- Some think the church exists to promote a specific denomination
- Some view the church as a charitable organization
- Some think the church is for weak people
- Some think it is a place for spiritual experiences or breakthroughs
- Some view it is a place where great messages are taught
- Some view it as a place of fellowship or a support system
- Some view it as something they are "supposed" to do as a Christian
- Some think it is a place to gain an identity or self-worth
- Some view the church as an organization that takes care of Christians and as a result remain inward focused

As I said before, not all of these are bad or wrong, but at the same time none of these viewpoints are the PRIMARY purpose of the church. The primary purpose is to raise saviors who can impact and transform the world with the values of the Kingdom of God. All of the above concepts are a means to an end. The church grows to gain influence, the church takes in the weak to make them strong, the church teaches the Word so it can be applied and lived out, the church ministers to its own so they can minister to others outside the four walls. Everything is focused beyond the church building, becoming externally focused, becoming the salt of the earth and the light of the world. This is the only way the church can pass through fire and receive a reward.

> *"According to the grace of God which is given unto me, as a wise master-builder, I have laid the foundation, and another buildeth thereon. But let every man take heed how he buildeth thereupon. For other foundation can no man lay than that is laid, which is Jesus Christ. Now if any man build upon this foundation gold, silver, precious stones, wood, hay, stubble; Every man's work shall be made manifest: for the day shall declare it, because it shall be revealed by fire; and the fire shall try every man's work of what sort it is If any man's work abide which he hath built thereupon, he shall receive a reward. If any man's work shall be burned, he shall suffer loss: but he himself shall be saved; yet so as by fire."(I Corinthians 3:10-15 KJV)*

Let churches lay the same foundation as Paul the Apostle, which is Jesus Christ. Churches must build according to the kingdom pattern and raise people who can be agents of change in the world for Christ. In addition, Christ-likeness must become the standard and expectation for every church member and leader. Only the work of the cross in ones heart can reveal the Christ of the cross to a lost generation. The cornerstone of the church is Jesus Christ and His life is like a torrent that should burst forth among the nations of this earth. It will take this supernatural life to change the world.

Too many things are being used to substitute the presence of God, which cannot be mechanized or formulized. Every tree is known by its fruit and, in the same way, every work is known by its results. It is time for the church to look at her fruit and to be courageous enough to examine the root.

## THE WORK AHEAD

> *"For as many [of you] as were baptized into Christ [into a spiritual union and communion with Christ, the Anointed One, the Messiah] have put on (clothe yourselves with) Christ." (Galatians 3:27 AMP)*

The word for "baptized" in the Greek is "baptizo" and means to immerse repeatedly. To understand this, think about the process of converting cucumbers into pickles. If a cucumber is placed into boiling water, the effects of this bring about a temporal change. It is a one-time immersion and the Greek word for it is "bapto." Now, if one immerses the same cucumber into a vinegar solution, it results in a permanent change. Christians must get so immersed in Jesus Christ that an actual metamorphosis takes place. This is a permanent transformation that begins with taking on the virtues and values of Christ. The Holy Spirit must impart the spirit of the cross, through the word of the cross, until believer's become messengers of the cross in practice. Only then will the power and life of the resurrected Christ flow through them and affect people's lives. Only an authentic work of the Holy Spirit in ones hearts can produce real results that have the power to change lives.

## RAISING SAVIORS AND KINGS

> *And saviors shall come up on mount Zion to judge the mount of Esau; and the kingdom shall be the Lord's."(Obadiah 1:21 KJV)*

As mentioned earlier, the primary purpose of the church is to raise, train and disciple believers who become saviors that can reach out and deliver humanity from futility and bondage. Nehemiah was raised as a savior. Paul was raised a savior to the gentile world (Galatians 2:8). All of the 120 disciples were raised as saviors. Jesus Christ was born a Savior.

> "And she shall bring forth a son, and thou shalt call his name JESUS: for he shall save his people from their sins." (Matthew 1:21 KJV)

> "…Where is he that is born King…" (Matthew 2:2 KJV)

> "… and shalt call his name Jesus…and he shall reign over the house of Jacob forever; and of his kingdom there shall be no end." (Luke 1:31-33 KJV)

> "…Thou sayest that I am King. To this end was I born, and for this cause came I into the world," (John 18:37 KJV)

Every Christian was born after the order of the Lord Jesus Christ as saviors and kings (Rev 5:9-10 KJV). Jesus was the firstborn among many brethren. As part of the royal family, Christians have the ability to carry the same power and authority that Jesus had while he walked the earth. This is why Christianity must move beyond identifying with certain "beliefs" and enter the realm of "becoming." Too many believers are taught more about acting like a Christian than how to become one in reality.

Many churches can be compared to prison facilities, where pastors are the wardens and members are the prisoners, being kept inside the four walls of the church. Instead of training and equipping people to become ministers in the marketplace, many people are limited to using their God-given gifts and abilities solely in the local church. Every member should serve in the local church, but this is considered "keeping-house," rather than authentic ministry.

People must be trained and released to serve God's purpose in the earth. This means to be trained in character development, the Word of God, and in the Great Commission. Releasing them does not mean they go off on their own. Training in the church is a lifelong journey, but pastors must help people discover their assignment on earth and give them the freedom to fulfill it. They must be discipled in the Great Commandment in order to obey the Great Commission, which is the discipleship of nations (Matt 28:18-20 KJV). It is establishing kingdom values that supplant the values of the world, in every sphere of society, until the kingdoms of this world become the kingdom of Christ.

## SALT'S RELEVANCE

Think about salt in a saltshaker. It has no relevance other than to be preserved. Its significance and value is seen only when it is poured out from the saltshaker. It has to be released into the "soup" of this world for its potential to work. The true impact of the church is not within her four walls, but outside where members are released to transform their respective spheres of influence. This is the kingdom pattern for relevance. Salt is meant to be poured out and poured into something, producing a chemical reaction that changes the state of a thing. Christians, the salt of the earth, become valuable when they take their rightful place as saviors in Zion.

## KINGDOM PRINCIPLES FOR EVERY LOCAL CHURCH

- Understand the Great Commandment concerning the Great Commission
- Understand the details of the Great Commission
- Learn how to raise God's people as saviors and kings
- Train people to see the world through the eyes of eternity
- Train them to use their gifts and lives for Christ alone
- Train them to seek the kingdom first
- Teach members how to discover their purpose in serving humanity

- Teach members how to take responsibility for a sphere of life
- Train people to own and take full responsibility of their callings
- Train them to understand systems (world systems vs. kingdom systems)
- Teach them how to develop their faith for taking cities for Christ
- Teach members value-systems, structures, and organized righteousness

## THE UKRAINE PHENOMENON

The Embassy of God church in Ukraine is a 21$^{st}$ century phenomenon. It is distinct in every way and is a beautiful example of how saviors are to be raised in Zion. The Embassy of God church can easily be a prototype of what God seeks to accomplish in His body around the world. This is a church where thousands of outcasts have become transformers within society. Former drug addicts, prostitutes, helpless and hopeless people who were once rejected are now change catalysts and assets to Ukraine's national transformation. From the moment a soul comes to Christ, a discipleship process transforms each member into a societal savior. These saviors are taught to reign as kings in their respective areas of influence.

What's more amazing is the depth of internal freedom these souls possess and the short amount of time it takes to transform them into world changers. Imagine a person who has been addicted to alcohol for more than 30 years becoming a notable leader within three months of salvation and manifesting the fruit of Christ-likeness. The entire church membership has been raised to carry a kingdom consciousness that leaves no room for complacency. They are taught from day one that they have a God-given purpose, and that purpose is to live for Christ and His kingdom. They are taught how to use their gifts and abilities to address societal problems with Biblical solutions. Even invalids have a ministry called "Life without Excuses." They do more for the kingdom of God in one year than most healthy believers do in their lifetime and this is due to the training they have received and their willingness to want to make a difference.

A church with this kind of mindset is unstoppable and its influence unending. This is why the Embassy of God Church in Ukraine has around 100,000 members, but impacts millions of people each and every day. They have achieved this through their understanding of the Great Commission. They understand that the church exists to disciple the nation and the Ukraine is being changed and affected every single day. Their emphasis has allowed them to displace worldly value-systems with the value-systems of God's kingdom. This church is truly a walking kingdom in the earth today. The good news is that every local church can maintain and increase their relevance by taking on a kingdom mindset and understanding the need to fulfill the Great Commission.

# Chapter 2
# HOW SALT WORKS IN A SOUP
## "KINGDOM PRINCIPLES FOR TRANSFORMING WORLD-SYSTEMS"

> *"And he said, bring me a new cruse, and put salt therein. And they brought it to him. And he went forth unto the spring of the waters, and cast the salt in there, and said, thus saith the LORD, I have healed these waters; there shall not be from thence any more death or barren land." (II Kings 2:20-21 KJV)*

The Lord healed and transformed the waters in the above scripture through salt, which was poured out into the spring of a dead and barren sea. When a person becomes a new creation in Christ, they become the salt of the earth; the salt that heals and transforms the world around them. Jesus said, *"Have salt in yourselves…" (Mark 9:50)*. Christians are to be poured out into the waters of this world to heal and transform it. They can preserve, restore and bring life to people through Jesus Christ.

The world lies in wickedness because the spirit of this world controls it. *"And the whole world around us is under the power of the evil one" (I John 5:19 KJV)*. The dead waters represent worldly values and structures. In Ezekiel 47, the waters of the Dead Sea produced death and decay. If Christians are not the salt, there is little hope for the world to be restored and brought to life in Christ Jesus.

> *"Who gave himself for our sins, that he might deliver us from this present evil world." (Galatians 1:4 KJV)*

> *"Wherein in time past ye walked according to the course of this world, according to the prince of the power of the air, the spirit that now worketh in the children of disobedience."(Ephesians 2:2 KJV)*

It is when salt (Christians) leave the saltshaker (the four walls) and go out into the world that their relevance is revealed. The significance of God's children is directly related to the impact, value, and transformation they bring into people's lives and their environment. Deep in the heart of every Christian is the desire to live beyond themselves. Every person who has God living in their heart knows that there is more to life, that there is a deeper purpose and meaning when compared to the level of life they are living. The truth is that it takes God working through people for them to see and become aware of all that God has placed on the inside. When people give out what they have, it unlocks the power of God within and makes room to receive more.

Elisha poured the salt and applied it at the very spring of the waters. The spring represents the root, the very source of the disease that was causing barrenness and death. Salt is meant to deal with the source and not just symptoms. There are roots to every world system that are hostile towards God and His values. Every member of Christ's body must understand that nothing happens until men take responsibility. The plight and condition of the earth should be a concern of every Christian. Pastors must release God's people and their God given abilities to serve the purposes of establishing His kingdom. God's original mandate for the first Adam is still in place: to take dominion over the earth. Jesus is still the first-born among many brethren (Rom 8:29). Jesus was born a Savior (Matt 1:21) and functioned as a King (John 18:37), and He also died to give birth to saviors (Oba 1:21) and kings (Rev 5:9-10). They are greatly needed in the world today.

## UNDERSTANDING WORLD SYSTEMS

> "... And the whole world is under the control of the evil one." (I John 5:19 NIV)

> "And the great dragon was cast out, that old serpent, called the Devil, and Satan, which deceiveth the whole world..." (Revelation 12:9 KJV)

If you told people in the world that they were under Satan's influence, they would not only disagree with you, but also think it utter foolishness. What must be understood is that there is a satanic agenda in place with the objective of making this world completely godless. There are forces at work, openly and behind the scenes, whose specific purpose is displacing Christ's rightful ownership of the earth and the people in it. Satan has built and established a value system that is antagonistic to the values of Christ, and mankind has been born into and conditioned by this system. The demonic structures erected by him, have captivated the minds of men and unknowingly controlled their belief-systems (2 Tim 2:26 KJV).

The truth is that the mind of Christ and the world stand directly opposed to one another (1 Cor. 2:12). The world tells us we are gods unto ourselves and Jesus says apart from me you can do nothing (John 15:5). The world tells us to preserve our lives; Jesus calls us to lay them down (Matt. 16:25). The spirit of this world does have dominion over unbelievers, but Christians are not immune from its influence. This spirit encourages people to continue in their natural condition. It wants to keep Christians stagnant, with little ability to affect their surroundings, and brings a false sense of comfort that keeps the Spirit of God from working in the areas where He has yet to renew them.

Many believers maintain the outward appearance of a Christian life: they go to church, live moral lives, and do good deeds in the community. However, the Word clearly states that to remain a friend to the world is to be an enemy of God (James 4:4). It reveals how the spirit of this world, or conformity to it, manifests itself. *"For all that is in the world, the lust of the flesh, and the lust of the eyes, and the pride of life, is not of the Father, but is of the world"* (1 John 2:16). The three chief forms of the spirit of the world can be seen in: (1) The craving for pleasure, or the desire to enjoy the world; (2) The craving for material things, or the desire to possess the world; and (3) The craving for recognition, or the desire to be honored in the world. All Christians must guard against these temptations, and it is only conformity to Jesus Christ that keeps one from conforming to the world.

## THE DOUBLE KINGDOM

*"And he said unto me, O Daniel, a man greatly beloved, understand the words that I speak unto thee, and stand upright: for unto thee am I now sent. And when he had spoken this word unto me, I stood trembling. Then said he unto me, Fear not, Daniel: for from the first day that thou didst set thine heart to understand and to chasten thyself before thy God, thy words were heard, and I am come for thy words. But the prince of the kingdom of Persia withstood me one and twenty days: but, lo, Michael, one of the chief princes, came to help me; and I remained there with the kings of Persia." (Daniel 10:11-13 KJV)*

The archangel Gabriel was sent by God to respond to Daniel's prayer, but was resisted in the heavenlies by the prince of the kingdom of Persia and the kings of Persia (Daniel 10:13). Please notice that the forces that resisted Gabriel were called the prince of the kings of the kingdom of Persia. These kings were demonic spirits that ruled the kingdom of Persia through the physical king, King Cyrus. This demonstrates how demonic spirits use those in authority to push the agenda of the kingdom of darkness.

*"In the third year of Cyrus king of Persia…"*

> *"In those days I Daniel was mourning three full weeks."*
> *(Daniel 10:1-2 KJV)*

These spirits were called the "kings of Persia" and they had either a prince or a captain. They were able to rule by influencing men and women in key positions of government. By injecting thoughts into their minds, a belief system was cultivated and it was through this mindset that decisions and actions were eventually enacted as the law of the land. These laws controlled behavior and behavior determined the culture and value system found within Persia. This pattern is most definitely still in operation today.

> *"Son of man, take up a lamentation upon the king of Tyrus ... Thus said the Lord God; Thou sealest up the sum, full of wisdom, and perfect in beauty. Thou have been in Eden the garden of God; every precious stone was thy covering ... the workmanship of thy tabrets and of thy pipes was prepared in thee in the day that thou wast created. Thou art the anointed cherub that covereth." (Ezekiel 28:12 KJV)*

The passage of scripture mentioned above speaks of Lucifer, who became Satan, and as Satan, is here described as the spirit king of Tyrus. He was the unseen demonic prince over this kingdom. Satan exercised his reign over Persia through his influence over the physical King of Tyrus along with the culture and values of its people. Satan is the god of this dark age, and He is known in scripture as the one who weakens, schools, and deceives the nations of the earth (Isaiah 14:12-16; Rev 12:9). This is known as the double kingdom, the invisible realm dominating what is visible. The purpose of their influence over nations is to take over the lawful reign of Jesus Christ. This has been the conflict and crisis of the ages (Luke 19:14) and it is achieved through influence.

This is how the double kingdom works. Demonic spirits gain access to the minds of important, powerful and influential people. It is then that these spirits introduce a philosophy of life which becomes a pre-dominate belief system. After this mindset is formed decisions, actions and laws are enacted and, implemented based on these belief-systems. These laws condition behavior, lifestyles and culture, which become the very values on which society is built, established and governed. As children are born into a particular system, they naturally take on its values and are conditioned by them, even though these structures repel the rule of Christ and the message of His Cross.

Each and every nation of the world is built upon seven social structures. They include politics/government, business/economics, education, arts & entertainment, religion, mass media and the family. No nation exists without these fundamental structures. They are the pillars that hold nations together. The enemy seeks to control all seven spheres by erecting a value system on which each social structure is built. By controlling these structures, which are demonic in nature, the people are conditioned by their values. As the next generation is raised, trained and schooled in this worldly value system, there is a specific intent to oust Christ from their very consciousness and lives.

China is an example of a nation whose seven structures are established on the value-systems of this world. The government controls every aspect of this country. The ideology of communism has been perpetuated and sustained throughout every institution and social structure. Christianity is seen as a fundamental threat, and therefore, must be controlled. The pastors of certain churches are chosen by the government and trained by the government on what to teach and what not to teach. These pastors are not born again and do not believe in the Lordship of Christ. They adhere to a strict set of rules and prison awaits those who dare break these rules. Through fear and intimidation, the nation, its people and its structures remain slaves to a communist ideology.

North Korea is another example of a nation under the bondage of communism. All types of measures are used to force, control and manipulate its citizens to conform to dangerous philosophies and anti-Christian ideologies. There is a total absence of freedom and people are considered property of the state. Its citizens are taught and indoctrinated into the worship of its leader as god and they are equally taught to live out their life's purposes for the nation's communist ideology. It's astounding how the minds of people can be so conditioned, that it determines their character, culture, and destiny as a nation. Millions and millions of people are now in bondage to the belief-system of one man. There are examples of this type of control throughout history, from the time of Nimrod and the tower of Babel, to others like Emperor Nero, Stalin of the U.S.S.R, and Hitler of Germany. To control a nation, an ideology has to permeate its structures and condition the mind of its citizens.

A nation without God's rule will disintegrate into emptiness. It will lead to death and decay. History has proven this over and over again. The true wealth of a nation is the wealth of its values. The values that sustain and build nations are those that have their source in Christ. Only nations built on the values of Christ and His Kingdom will last. This is the fundamental reason why civilizations over the centuries rise and fall. A nation without the values of the kingdom of Christ is faulty and subject to decay.

## THE FALL OF THE KINGDOMS OF THIS WORLD

*"Thou, O king, art a king of kings: for the God of heaven hath given thee a kingdom, power, and strength, and glory. And wheresoever the children of men dwell, the beasts of the field and the fowls of the heaven hath he given into thine hand, and hath made thee ruler over them all. Thou art this head of gold. And after thee shall arise another kingdom inferior to thee, and another third kingdom of brass, which shall bear rule over all the earth. And the fourth kingdom shall be strong as iron: forasmuch as iron breaketh in pieces and subdueth all things: and as iron that breaketh all these, shall it break in pieces and bruise. And whereas thou sawest the feet and toes, part of potters' clay, and*

> *part of iron, the kingdom shall be divided; but there shall be in it of the strength of the iron, forasmuch as thou sawest the iron mixed with miry clay. And as the toes of the feet were part of iron, and part of clay, so the kingdom shall be partly strong, and partly broken And whereas thou sawest iron mixed with miry clay, they shall mingle themselves with the seed of men: but they shall not cleave one to another, even as iron is not mixed with clay And in the days of these kings shall the God of heaven set up a kingdom, which shall never be destroyed: and the kingdom shall not be left to other people, but it shall break in pieces and consume all these kingdoms, and it shall stand for ever Forasmuch as thou sawest that the stone was cut out of the mountain without hands, and that it brake in pieces the iron, the brass, the clay, the silver, and the gold; the great God hath made known to the king what shall come to pass hereafter: and the dream is certain, and the interpretation thereof sure." (Daniel 2:37-45 KJV)*

The scriptures above clearly show that the kingdoms of this world will come to an end. The reason is that their value systems are demonically influenced. Daniel 2 lists the various kingdoms that have fallen in times past. Here are the kingdoms: the head of gold represents the Babylonian kingdom; the arms and chest of silver represent the Persian kingdom; the belly and thighs of brass represent the Grecian kingdom; the leg of iron represents the Roman kingdom; and the feet of iron and clay represent the nations of the 21$^{st}$ century. These nations are partly strong and partly broken (Daniel 2:42), yet the clay is called the "potter's clay" in verse 41, indicating that there is a molding or conditioning taking place.

> *"And whereas thou sawest iron mixed with miry clay, they shall mingle themselves with the seed of men: but they shall not cleave one to another, even as iron is not mixed with clay." (Daniel 2:43 KJV)*

There is a personality behind the creation of the clay feet in this great image. The weakness of these kingdoms is in their values, and the values destroying the nations of the earth are orchestrated by demonic influences, hence, the potter's clay. Satan is known as one who weakens the nations (Isaiah 14:16); He is the potter who is molding the clay. The stone that was cut out of the mountain represents Jesus Christ, the Chief Cornerstone.

> "Wherefore also it is contained in the scripture, Behold, I lay in Zion a chief corner stone, elect, precious: and he that believeth on him shall not be confounded." (I Peter 2:6 KJV).

The mountain represents Zion, the church of the Living God. This stone will destroy the kingdoms that are influenced by Satan and consume it (Revelation 11:15), but at the same time dominate and fill the earth (Daniel 2:34-35) with the presence of the King and His values.

> "But the saints of the Most High shall take the kingdom, and possess the kingdom for ever, even for ever and ever" (Daniel 7:18 KJV)

As the salt of the earth, Christians have a responsibility to reclaim the nations of the earth for Christ by uprooting these demonic systems.

> "Ye are the salt of the earth: but if the salt has lost his savor, wherewith shall it be salted? It is thenceforth good for nothing, but to be cast out, and to be trodden under foot of men." (Matthew 5:13 KJV)

It is time for the body of Christ to take responsibility for the earth. It is time for her to rise up and take her place as the mountain established above all other mountains. God is depending on His church to reconcile the world back to Him, and it is very possible to reclaim territory for the Kingdom of God. It is by understanding how salt works that kingdom principles for transforming world-systems will become clear and its application will become a reality.

> *"And the men of the city said unto Elisha, Behold, I pray thee, the situation of this city is pleasant, as my lord seeth: but the water is naught, and the ground barren. And he said, Bring me a new cruse, and put salt therein. And they brought it to him. And he went forth unto the spring of the waters, and cast the salt in there, and said, Thus saith the LORD, I have healed these waters; there shall not be from thence any more death or barren land." II Kings 2:19-21 KJV)*

## KINGDOM PRINCIPLES FOR TRANSFORMING WORLD-SYSTEMS

### PRINCIPLE I: GET THE SALT OUT OF THE SHAKER

Christians must get out of the four walls of the church and into the marketplace. This is the only way they will reclaim their value, significance and influence in the world. Salt must be poured out into all seven spheres of society. Remember, the church exists as a tool to accomplish a greater purpose. It is a training center where saviors and kings are raised to fulfill their God-given assignments. Every member of the body of Christ should be raised and released as saviors of the earth. The relevance of salt is directly connected to earth's issue and this is why believers are called the salt of the earth. This is why leaders have a responsibility to train God's people to address the ills of society and bring God's righteousness and justice into all aspects of culture. Just as God told Pharaoh, "Let my people go that they may serve me," it is time to release people to fulfill the mandate of God outside the church building.

What is often called ministry, such as ushering, singing, greeting, and preaching is really not ministry. What is done inside a local church is necessary and vital to the life of a church, but it is not what

Jesus considered ministry. The work of the ministry referred to in Ephesians 4, is ministry outside the four walls of the church. The things done inside church are simply to maintain or keep the house functional, so that its primary objective can be carried out without any impediment. This objective is the discipleship of nations or the Great Commission. The question, therefore, that needs to be asked is, "are the activities, programs, efforts and direction of our churches all focused toward fulfilling the Great Commission?" This will be the litmus test of the true 21$^{st}$ century church.

Compare this to how salt works. Everyone has saltshakers at home on a dining table or in their kitchens. Salt is used to season and bring flavor to food. Even so, the power of salt is not when it's in the shaker, but when it is poured out of its container and into a soup or a meal. In fact, salt is purchased with the sole objective of being poured out. In the same way, the church is not to keep people in the four walls, but to send them out to accomplish the work of the Great Commission. If the church hoards God's greatest asset (people), it will naturally undermine the work of the Great Commission.

The lack of training and equipping the church to take their place within the seven societal structures is the very reason the condition of the earth is what it is today. God is going to hold Christians responsible for this. Pastors need to ask themselves some questions: Am I a contributor to the condition of the earth and humanity in the world today? Have I fallen short of God's test and assignment for the 21$^{st}$ century church? Am I willing to part with wrong conceptions and do everything within my power to change? It is time to give God's people back to God to be used for His glory. May every pastor's eyes be opened to see the bigger picture of Christ's death and His reason for establishing the church. All of His work stands on the call to fulfill the Great Commission as a means to establishing His reign in the earth.

## PRINCIPLE II: THE SALT MUST ENTER INTO THE SOUP

The church must engage the systems of this world and not be afraid of the culture or its influence. God wants His church actively involved in today's culture, not isolated from it. Christians are called to be big players in the marketplace, not standing on the sidelines (Matt 11:16-17). To change a system, believers must get into it, to transform it, without conforming to it. This only happens by understanding a specific system and how it works. God used Moses, who grew up in an Egyptian system, to deliver a people bound by its system. Jesus used disciples who grew up in a Jewish system, to bring in the kingdom system within the same system. God delivered the Apostle Paul from a people and a system and sent him back to it (Acts 26:13-16). The church should not remain primitive in her thinking. She is in the world for a reason - to transform it and impose the kingdom of God. Raise people up and with the intent to strategically plant them into the seven spheres of society. It is from within that change is possible, and not from without. Even God knew that to change the world and its values, He had to become a part of it by taking on the nature of a man (Heb 2:14 & Phil 2:5-9).

Once again be reminded that the church must understand that the Great Commission has to do with the discipleship of nations. Structures are the pillars on which nations are established, and whoever controls the value-system of each individual structure controls the nation. These seven structures are: politics/government, business/economics, education, arts & entertainment, religion, mass media and the family. Each of these structures is built upon the value-system of Christ or the value-system of this world. It is good to take some time and think about each structure in ones nation and the value-system they possess. The success of a church should be measured by the impact made within each structure and not by the size of a particular church or network.

Salt is poured out with a definite purpose in mind. It is designed to season food, and nothing of value happens until it is poured out. This is the only way it works; it is the only way it brings change to food. Following this same principle, Christians have to enter the systems of this world in order to change them. If they only stay in the religious and family structures, there is no possibility of change within the other five structures. Take a look at government leaders today. How many of them are Christians that function like Daniel or Joseph? Some churches believe that Christians should be occupied with winning souls and not be bothered at all with political affairs. These are the ones who need a fresh understanding of the Great Commission.

God Himself adopted this principle by becoming the "Word made Flesh." He knew that in order to change the world, He had to become a part of its system. No, He did not descend from heaven on chariots of fire, nor did He come down in the blazing light of the sun. He took on flesh and blood and became human. He underwent the same process of natural birth and was born into the world. Before He asked us to become like Him, He decided to become like us, in order to identify and fully understand us. He knew that in order to change the system, He must enter into it and change it from within.

Imagine Jesus Christ trying to change the world without first becoming a part of it. The church is not about "in-house" activities on a given Sunday, but about the impact she makes outside the four walls from Monday through Saturday. It is about identifying callings and how these callings are harnessed to transform various spheres of life. To change a nation, change her seven structures, get into it and raise people up with the intention of planting them, using the values of God, which are far superior in nature to that of this world, to establish His kingdom in the earth.

In order for this to happen, a new paradigm shift must be embraced in the way church is carried out. Secondly, pastors must raise each member as a savior whose relevance is dependent on the impact she or he brings to their sphere of influence. Next, divide the church into seven units for the sole purpose of raising people whose gifts and callings are relational to one or more of these seven structures. Church leaders must become intentional in raising people to enter into these structures and become agents of change.

This is why the church must become dynamic both spiritually and academically. Members must study the systems of this world and understand how they operate and function. They should become experts in various fields, so that, at anytime, they can bring relevance to a nation's life. To become successful at anything, one must master the intended subject. Think of money as an example. Many honorable Christians are poor or only able to take care of their own family. Many have been taught about finances only in regards to tithes and offerings, yet there is so much more to wealth creation than tithes and offerings. There is simply no way to change ones financial situation without understanding money and how it works. So the Christians must speak the "language" of each particular field and through the operation of God's wisdom, communicate the gospel of the kingdom.

## PRINCIPLE III: SALT LOSES ITS OUTWARD SHELL

Salt is easily identified by its color or outward look but it is bought and used only for its effect.

> *"...That they may see your good works, and glorify your Father which is in heaven" (Matt 5:16)*

> *"If I do not the works of, my father, believe me not. But if I do, though ye believe not me, believe the works: that ye may know, and believe, that the Father is in me, and I in him" (John 10:37-38 KJV)*

Think about when salt is used in the kitchen. When seasoning a meal, it loses its white crystalline color upon saturation. This is an important principle in the life of a Christian in regards to transforming nations. Take a look at the following principles:

- Every nation or society is built on seven fundamental structures
- These structures are: (a) Government (b) Business (c) Education (d) Mass Media (e) Arts and Entertainment (f) Religion (g) Family
- Each of these structures is built on a value-system

- Every value-system is sourced in either God or Satan
- The predominant value-system reveals who is in control
- Nations are controlled by the beliefs of its value-system
- To transform a nation or society, its values must be changed

The reason the church has yet to gain influence is because she's held on to her crystalline color. Somehow, consciously or unconsciously, it is easy for Christians to remain locked up in the "world" of religion at the expense of the other six worlds. This means that the church is 1/7 relevant but 6/7 irrelevant. One of the ways this is clearly visible is through denominations, which are simply external labels. These labels are often with good intentions, as a means to protect the rights and beliefs of a particular Christian group. However, this moves us away from the simplicity that is found in Christ and focuses on minor differences. Doctrine is vitally important, but the point is, the world doesn't care about it. Revisit the book of Acts, and ask, "What did they preach?" The emphasis was Christ – they preached Christ to the lost, not doctrines. These external labels often cloud the true purpose of the church by making the church the focus, instead of the kingdom. The church is simply a means to an end, which is the reign of Christ and the reign of His values in the earth.

Another point worthy of consideration is the fact that different laws govern each of these "worlds". The world of "Business" is very different from that of "Family," and that of "Government" is different from "Religion." This is why the laws of religion have no impact on other worlds. In order to become effective in transforming nations, Christians have to apply the appropriate laws to the right sphere (Acts 9:19-23). The world is not concerned about external identifications and will never be won over by them. The same principle applies to salt. It is bought and used only because of its power and not for its color. Religious clichés turn the world away from Christ. External labeling has done nothing to transform a nation. To win the world, believers must come back to the simplicity that is found in Christ.

Let the world see the Gospel in action rather than hearing claims or opinions.

The usefulness of salt lies in its transformational ability, therefore, the relevance of Christians is found in the impact they make in bringing transformation into the structures of society. God lived in a different world than ours. He lived in inapproachable light and in a dimension governed by a different set of laws. God moved out of time into time and repackaged Himself in human flesh. He left His realm and came into ours, and as a baby, was no different externally than any other child. Imagine the lengths that God took in order to fully identify with the human race. He left His divine attributes (Phil 2:6-7) and took on the natural form of a man. It's another way of saying that He lost His crystalline color, in order to become one with the system He came to change.

## PRINCIPLE IV: SALT TAKES ON THE NATURE OF THE SOUP

When salt is poured into a pot of soup, it loses its outward color and takes on the nature of the soup. It actually takes on the nature of whatever it is poured into and not vice versa. This is a very powerful principle. Salt takes on the nature of whatever it is poured into and becomes one with it, just as Christ took on the nature of man and became one with man. What does this mean? Christians cannot change a system or structure without identifying with the system first. Jesus became one with the system in order to identify and understand the system. His sole objective was to bring change to the system. How can one change the business sphere, with no training in business? To change a system, one must understand how it works. Sitting back and complaining about the entertainment industry is not going to accomplish anything worthwhile, until individuals understand it and then seek to transform it. Too many people have left the political world while hoping and praying that things would change, yet the Word of God clearly states that when the righteous are in authority, the people rejoice (Proverb 29:2). The true power of the church takes place as we engage the systems of this world.

Identifying with the world is a necessity, but identification does not mean compromising, nor does it mean conformity. It simply means becoming a master of their systems with the underlining aim to influencing and transforming it. Think about trying to communicate with a foreigner whose language you cannot understand. This would get frustrating. Understanding and speaking the language would establish common grounds for communication. This is what Christians must do in each structure of a nation. For example, if a person is a scientist, they are more likely to relate with and influence a group of scientists.

This is why the concept of church must change if today's church is to bring change. Imagine each person in your church being trained to use their lives, gifts, and resources to enter, identify, understand, master, influence and transform a sphere or structure. Jesus mastered each sphere of His day and one only need to read His parables to understand how He used the language of His time to communicate His message. He spoke of investment, banking, agriculture, winemaking, fiscal responsibility, the weather, political systems and structures, leadership, responsibility and accountability, work ethic, construction, etc. In fact, none of His disciples were from the religious sector but were all from the marketplace. Salt must loose its outward shell and color in order to become one with the world it enters.

## PRINCIPLE V: SALT DIES TO LIVE

> *"Always bearing about in the body the dying of the Lord Jesus, that the life also of Jesus might be made manifest in our body. For we which live are always delivered unto death for Jesus' sake, that the life also of Jesus might be made manifest in our mortal flesh So then death worketh in us, but life in you." (II Corinthians 4:10-12 KJV)*

Salt that is poured into soup dies to live. It dies to release quickening power. Think about how a pinch of salt alters an entire pot of soup and compare it to how Christians living a salted life gives power to bring transformation.

## UNDERSTANDING THE LIFE THAT QUICKENS

*"Verily, verily, I say unto you, except a corn of wheat fall into the ground and die, it abideth alone: but if it die, it bringeth forth much fruit. He that loveth his life shall lose it; and he that hateth his life in this world shall keep it unto life eternal." (John 12:24-25 KJV)*

It is the "much fruit" (in terms of power of productivity) that must be comprehended in the death-life of Christ. The life force within the seed remains imprisoned until the shell holding that life breaks away through death. The death of the outer shell releases the life of the seed with compound productivity. The life of God in the inner-man remains imprisoned until the shell of the self-life dies. "Life flowing out of death," therefore, becomes a principle of the kingdom. Remember that that inner life is a torrent (John 7:38), and not a strain. The greatest barrier to the outflow of God's life within us all is the self-life of this world. *"For whosoever will save his life shall lose it: and whosoever will lose his life for my sake shall find it," (Matt 16:25 KJV).* This inner life of God's Spirit is the power that quickens *"for it is the Spirit that gives life" (John 6:63).*

## THE DEATH OF CHRIST

The death of Christ is no ordinary death; it is immortal dying. It contains within itself, like a seed, the energy of a new organic life force. *"Thou fool, that which thou sowest is not quickened, except it die" (1Cor 15:36 KJV).* Jesus, through death; gave life to all who appropriate it by faith. *"That if one died for all, and that he died for all, that they which live shall no longer live unto themselves" (II Cor. 5:14-15 KJV).*

The death of a seed relives its life in nine hundred more, and nine hundred in a million. In the same way, Christ relives His life in millions of people. Christians are planted together with Him; a union brought about by the Holy Spirit. They are engrafted to become partakers of a vital union and raised in practice with resurrection life (Romans 6:3-5). It is the life of Christ that quickens. In order to become productive in the kingdom, His quickening life must permeate the world and quicken it with the life of Christ. The more one dies; the more they live. Therefore, more life is needed to die; and more death to live.

*"So, then death works in us, but life in you" (II Co. 4:12).* Paul the Apostle said, "I die daily." The deeper the death in Christ, the more forceful the quickening power of Christ will flow and transform the world. "In Him is life and this life is the light of the world." The church is filled with people who have not been taught the concept of death, or the work of the cross in severing the believer from all that hinders the spirit life in the inner-man. Only the work of the cross will reveal the Christ of the cross. The cross not only brings believers to the living Savior but also, severs them from the effects of the old life, which is, the impact of sin in the soul. This same cross severs not only the dominion of sin (II Col 2:11-12), but also the appetites of the flesh (Gal 5:24), the influence of the world (Gal 6:14), from demonic influences (John 12:31; 14:30), and from self.

> *"Whosoever will come after me, let him deny himself, and take up his cross, and follow me. For whosoever will save his life shall lose it; but whosoever shall lose his life for my sake and the gospel's, the same shall save it."* (Mark 8:34-35 KJV)

> *"And Satan answered the LORD, and said, Skin for skin, yea, all that a man hath will he give for his life." (Job 2:4 KJV)*

All Christians need to be saved from self: self-pity, self-preservation, self-love, self-importance, self-vindication, self-interest and self-centeredness. Christ lived and moved through Paul, because Christ became his fixed center. It is this work of the cross that will reveal the Christ of the cross to the world. This is the power that many churches have no concept of and as a result, remain powerless to win the world back to God. The pure life of the spirit cannot be mechanized or formulized; it must be wrought in us by a true work of the Holy Spirit. Review the following points as major keys to the transformation of societies and nations.

- God's work is either enhanced or limited by the depth of His work in the believer
- God can only do through a person what He has done in them
- There is a spiritual component to the transformation of nations
- Every genuine transformation is directly influenced by the Holy Spirit
- Only as one dies to self can God's power to transform flow
- The Christian life must translate into the values and character of Christ just as the life of the vine translates into tangible fruit
- Only as living epistles can Christians become the message in reality.

The power to transform the world is sourced in the power of God's Spirit and this power, like a river, enters into the dead sea of this world to heal and transform it. Only as Christians die to self will that same power quicken everything it touches. Tincture a glass of water with a drop of ink and the entire glass of water is transformed. Let's sink deep into the death of Christ so that more of His life can flow and touch the world, herein lies the secret of Christianity to transform people and nations.

## PRINCIPLE VI: SALT PERMEATES THE ENTIRE SOUP

When salt is poured into soup, it subtly infiltrates the entire pot of soup. This speaks of God's wisdom in transforming the nations of the world. Wisdom is not just a vital key but it is the main key in transforming nations into a kingdom culture. When speaking of wisdom, it refers to a well thought-out strategy on how to take cities for Christ. Accessing God's wisdom must be a priority in the believer's life. The book "Accessing the Wisdom of God" by Dr. Sunday Adelaja is a must read in regards to obtaining wisdom.

> *"And he by his wisdom delivered the city …then said I, wisdom is better than strength" (Ecclesiastes 9:14-16 KJV)*

## WISDOM TO CHANGE VALUE-SYSTEMS

The human nature inherited from the first Adam (Acts 17:26) is corrupt both in root and branch. It can only be re-created in Christ (II Corinthians 5:17). This fundamental flaw will naturally lead to the demise of a nation's failure and ruin. Value-systems shape a nation's culture and determine its success or failure. Even within a family unit, a child's destiny is largely determined by the value-system that was modeled before him or her. Think about the educational system of a nation. By controlling what students study, their programs, curriculums and syllabus, you control much of their belief-system, which directly affects their destiny. Through education, Satan entrenches his value system deep into the minds of people.

These values ultimately determine belief systems and behavior, as well as the destiny of a nation and its people. Therefore, whoever controls the value-system controls the nation and its destiny. Satan understands this principle and fights to keep nations bound to his will in this way. Is it surprising then to see the world's antagonistic behavior and outspoken hatred towards Christ, His followers and His cause? In America, there is a pagan religion pretending to be no religion at all. It does everything within its power to push its own agenda, which is hostile to Christ and His values. It insists upon doing away with the fundamental beliefs of the Christian faith by simultaneously promoting its own religion. Its true purpose is to displace the reign of Christ from society. Their aim is to make America Christ-less.

## OUR TRUE MISSION AS SALT OF THE EARTH

*"Go then and make disciples of all the nations."* (Matthew 28:19 AMP)

The command to disciple nations is the mandate of the church. To disciple a nation means to bring the rule of God's government into the structures upon which a society is built. It means to bring the character of the King and the values of His kingdom into the seven spheres of a nation's life. If the gospel is to have maximum impact, then the satanic values in the world must be displaced. Until the gospel addresses the societal ills of a nation, the church falls short in fulfilling her divine mandate. Christians are to transform all sectors of a nation with the values and character of Christ. Then they can say that the kingdoms of this world have become the kingdom of their God and of His Christ.

## ADAM'S EXAMPLE

God intentionally chose Adam's place of abode. It was a place built upon divine blueprints and kingdom values, a place that was a prototype of God's abode in the heavens.

*In the beginning God created the heavens and the earth."* (Genesis 1:1 KJV)

Just as man was created in the image of God (Gen 1:26), the earth was created to reflect the heavens. The earth is actually part of the heavens as a planet suspended in space. Through Adam, God's image, one can see into God's realm and character, and through the earth, one understands the God's dwelling place in the heavens.

> *"And the LORD God planted a garden eastward in Eden; and there he put the man whom he had formed." (Genesis 2:8 KJV)*

Man's creation was important to God and so was his environment. Adam was to live in the garden and ultimately make the entire earth look like Eden.

> *"And the LORD God took the man and put him into the Garden of Eden to dress it and to keep it." (Genesis 2:15 KJV)*

Man was to take full responsibility for the Garden of Eden and to transform the entire earth after its pattern.

> *"And they heard the sound of the Lord God walking in the garden in the cool of the day, and Adam and his wife hid themselves from the presence of the Lord God among the trees of the garden." (Genesis 3:8 AMP)*

The Garden of Eden was a place where God Himself came into fellowship with man as a partner over the affairs of the earth. Everyone and everything needs the right atmosphere to thrive. The earth, as God's footstool, is His resting place and Satan should not be allowed to usurp God's resting place, that is, His reign over the earth. When Adam fell, his fall affected not only his spirit, soul and body, but also creation as a whole (Romans 8:20-22). Satan found an in-road into the earth realm and brought his value system (Romans 5:12). As generation after generations were born into the world, their belief-systems were shaped by pre-existing norms, values, and cultures of the day. When Jesus Christ came on the scene; He brought with Him a new-order. *"From that time Jesus began to preach, and to say, Repent: for the kingdom of heaven is at hand" (Matthew 4:17 KJV)*. He came to destroy and displace the existing culture and replace it with the kingdom of God.

> *"... The land is as the garden of Eden before them."*
> *(Joel 2:3 KJV)*

The earth must once again become as the Garden of Eden. In order to achieve this, the church must intentionally raise people like the Joseph, Daniel and Esther and prepare them for positions of influence in every sector of society. Through a superior operation of God's wisdom, they will bring in the values of the kingdom and provide solutions to global problems in the world, e.g. the cure for cancer. When the answers to global issues are found to be in the hands of the church, the world will look to the church and submit to the wisdom of God.

## PRINCIPLE VII: SALT TRANSFORMS THE ENTIRE SOUP

It is through a complex chemical reaction that salt changes the entire outcome of a meal. Although it takes on the nature of the soup, it is the soup that gets transformed by the power of salt. It is a true picture of how systems are changed from the inside out. Salt penetrates into every structure of a meal and transforms its internal structure. This is its intent and design. Remember that the one fundamental reason why nations fall is because human nature is inherently corrupt and its cure lies in being re-created in Christ. This is why the prophecy in the book of Daniel 2, clearly reveals the irrefutable truth, which is: "All the kingdoms of men must fall, and only the kingdom of Christ will stand." This is not a mystery but a true scientific fact that has well-documented historical facts to validate the rise and fall of nations. If one carefully follows the principle shown in 2 Kings 2: 19-22, they would observe the actions of the salt life in its ability to transform values from the root.

1. Salt reaches saturation at 26.4% per room temperature. This means that it takes time to penetrate systems and structures. Patience must be exercised in training up people to strategically enter societal structures. To be most effective,

each member would need to be trained to give their life to addressing one or more spheres.

2. Salt alters the entire outcome of a soup, due to a complex chemical reaction. Its molecules are able to penetrate into every ingredient and transform its very composition. In the new birth, the spirit of man is recreated in Christ, thus quickening, rearranging and completely altering its very nature. Likewise, salt alters soup at the cellular level by changing its very nature into something irreversibly different. Christians are to bring transformation, in both root and branch, to every sector of a nation's life. Real transformation requires that Christians understand the root-causes of societal ills, eradicate them, and in their place establish new systems that will sustain lasting posterity.

3. The process of transformation will take place when the church comprehends the message of the Great Commission, also known as the "gospel of the kingdom." It is the gospel of the government of Christ in and over all things. It begins in the hearts and minds of men and spreads out to all aspects of creation. His rule in their hearts gives them a new nature and His rule in their minds gives them a new mindset.

## KINGDOM PRINCIPLES FOR RAISING TRANSFORMATIONAL LEADERS

- Christians must understand that the local church is the training ground where saviors are raised
- All saviors must pursue the goal of becoming more like Christ
- They must know that their purpose in life has to be discovered
- They must understand that their calling relates to a specific sphere of society
- Saviors must understand the value-system of the sphere they choose to change

- They must strive to be the best in their field of influence as a platform to establishing kingdom values
- Saviors must access the wisdom of God on how to bring the kingdom of God into all aspects of society

# Chapter 3
# THE TWO MAIN FUNCTIONS OF SALT
## "KINGDOM RESPONSIBILITIES OF A BELIEVER"

*"Nothing happens in the earth until men take responsibility"- Sino Agueze*

### UNDERSTANDING KINGDOM RESPONSIBILTY

*"For unto us a child is born, unto us a son is given: and the government shall be upon his shoulder...Of the increase of his government and peace, there shall be no end, upon the throne of David, and upon his Kingdom, to order it, and to establish it with judgment and with justice from henceforth even forever. The zeal of the Lord of hosts will perform this" (Isaiah 9:6-7 KJV)*

### FOR UNTO US A CHILD IS BORN

*"For unto you is born this day in the City of David a savior, which is Christ the Lord." (Luke 2:11 KJV)*

Every person reaches a point when they ask, "What is the meaning of life?" or "Why am I here; what is my purpose?" The above scriptures reveal that Jesus is the Father's gift to the world, and He was given for the benefit of all humanity. He was born for a people, for the goodwill of all creation. Not only do these prophecies speak of Christ, they also speak of every Christian, every believer that is alive today (Isaiah 53:10). Christ-followers were born into this world for a people, the crown of God's creation. They serve God by serving people. There are millions of people waiting for God's children to rise up and bring to them the message of the gospel. It is a message that is full of power, and this power is activated when it is spoken and transmitted when it is received. Awake to the assignment God has for the church. God has plans and purposes that need to be established in the earth, and He is counting on His body. Jesus said, *"As the Father sent me into the world, even so have I also sent you into the world."* (John 17:18 KJV)

> *"Before I formed thee in the belly I knew thee; and before thou camest forth out of the womb I sanctified thee, and I ordained thee a prophet unto the nations."* (Jeremiah 1:5 KJV)

This verse proves that a divine assignment has been established for every believer's life. There is no one in the kingdom of God who is ordinary. There is a seed of greatness on the inside of every citizen. It is not reserved for a select few, but for every child of God. There is an assignment; there is purpose and a beautiful future waiting for all who allow God to work in and through them.

## TRAIN UP A CHILD

> *"Train up a child in the way he should go and when he is old, he will not depart from it. The rich ruleth over the poor, and the borrower is servant to the lender."* (Proverbs 22:6-7 KJV)

Parents have a responsibility to raise godly children for Him and for the cause of His kingdom (Genesis. 18:17-19). They are to help their children discover their purpose and to raise them accordingly. Children can be raised rich or poor, as rulers or slaves and as lenders or borrowers. There are two distinct ways that can ensure one's child fulfills the plan of God for their life.

**I. Raise them rich in Christ:** *"So is he that layeth up treasure for himself and is not rich toward God" (Luke 12:21 KJV).* Children should be taught that God is the richest treasure they could ever possess. Establish them in the fundamentals of the Christian faith. Train them how to seek God's face with their whole heart. They must learn how to abide in the Vine, let the word of Christ dwell in them richly, and to know the Holy Spirit as a person. The most effective way for a parent to teach their children is to model this life before them. They should be able to see the beatitudes and kingdom values lived out on a daily basis. They should see character and integrity on display. Parents set up their children for success when they help them discover God's plan for their lives and show them how to develop into living purposefully for Christ.

**II. Raise them up as rulers:** *"Thou sayest that I am a king. To this end was I born, and for this cause came I into the world" (John 18:34 KJV).* Every person can reign as a ruler or king through the authority of Jesus Christ. Christians are kings by birthright (Revelation 5:10), and this means that they are called to rule in at least one of the seven spheres of a society's life. Children can be effectively trained to rule by parents teaching them who they are in Christ Jesus. This will mold their hearts and minds in a way that prepares them to live out kingdom character and values that reveal the nature of their King. These values can be displayed during school, sport activities and in the treatment of others. They will be carried into adolescence and college, until they reach adulthood and become assets to their community and the kingdom of God.

> *"I have coveted no man's silver, or gold, or apparel. Yea, ye yourselves know, that these hands have ministered unto my necessities and to them that were with me. I have showed you all things, how that so laboring ye ought to support the weak, and to remember the words of the Lord Jesus, how he said, it is more blessed to give than receive." (Acts 20:33-35 KJV)*

God will hold parents responsible for how they raise and train their children. Children are a gift from God and are entrusted to the care of parents. Discipline is rarely necessary when children are trained right. They can be taught; in whatever they do, to have an excellent spirit. They can learn about dignity of labor and the results of hard work. Parents, not schools or churches, are to teach them personal responsibility, relational skills, leadership skills, money skills, and life-skills. *"Unto us a son is given: and the government shall be upon his shoulder."* Every child has been given to reach a people and parents can ensure they succeed in this divine plan. Children are able to develop into and possess a kingdom mindset. As they grow into maturity they will be able to grow into sons of God and deliver a sphere of society. The government of God is only placed on the shoulder of sons, because only a son has the capacity to carry out kingdom objectives with grace and wisdom.

> *"… Necessity is laid upon me; yea, woe is unto me, if I… a dispensation of the gospel is committed unto me."* (1 Corinthians 9:16-17 KJV)

Paul the Apostle understood the enormity of his assignment and the kingdom responsibility that was placed upon His shoulders. He took full responsibility for his God-given assignment as though all of heaven depended on Him. Paul wanted to please the Father and to finish the race strong. He guarded what was entrusted to Him with His life. Now is the time for the church to no longer see themselves as workers, but those who are sent to a people; those who have a responsibility to cities and nations. This was how the primitive church shook the world for Christ (Acts 17:6).

## WHY AM I ALIVE?
## THE QUESTION OF PURPOSE

The question of "why am I alive" has to do with ones life purpose. It deals with the reason a person exists on planet Earth. It's about discovering the intent of the Creator in His creation of a person. There is nothing created by God that is without purpose. Just look around: birds were created to fly; the sun was created to give light; plants were designed to give life, etc. God is a God of purpose and design and humanity is not exempt as His creation.

## GOD HAD A PLAN BEFORE YOU WERE BORN

*"I knew you before I formed you in your mother's womb. Before you were born I set you apart and appointed you as my prophet to the nations." (Jeremiah 1:5 NLT)*

Many Christians are not aware that God has a special and unique plan for their life. It's a "one of a kind" plan, something designed before their parents even conceived. God's desire for His children is so beyond the frame of their natural minds, and more often than not, bigger than they can ever comprehend. *"For I know the plans I have for you, says the LORD. They are plans for good and not for disaster, to give you a future and a hope." (Jeremiah 29:11 NLT)* This scripture alone is the exact reason why people should seek God for direction in every area of their lives and not to lean on their own understanding. To find ones purpose, they should go to the source. They should learn to sit in the presence of God and draw close to Him with their whole heart. The more a person seeks after God, the more He reveals Himself and His plans for his or her life. God never reveals the full picture in one day, but rather unfolds it day by day, as one walks in communion with Him. God is a responsible Father, and the believer's part is to walk by faith each day in order to live out their purpose. This is the reason why they must practice His presence as a means to staying connected to Him at all times.

## LIFE IS A GIFT OF TRUST - A PRIVILEGE & A LOAN

There are only three things one can choose to do with their life: (1) spend it, (2) waste it, or (3) invest it. If understood, this personal choice is what will equip believers to live whole-heartedly for God. What is God's view on life? How does He see the days and years lived out on earth? Life is a gift of trust. Every person is a steward of his or her life and will give account for how it is used. Life is more than going to school, getting married, buying a house, having children and making a living. These are good things, but they are not the cores of why humanity exists. Life is about living for Christ and the cause of His kingdom. God knows these other things are important, but He says, "Seek ye first the kingdom of God." This approach to life is the true secret to experiencing the abundant life. Pastor Sunday says, "God treats everyone the same, but not everyone treats God the same." This is so true. Those who hold nothing back from God will experience God holding nothing back from them. When people settle in their hearts what living on earth means to them and are able to view life through the eyes of eternity, they are sure to experience it on a different level. The cares of this world will not consume them. They will see a deeper meaning behind life's challenges and triumphs. Their focus and determination to live single-mindedly for Christ will cause them to be very effective and fruitful in the kingdom.

## WHY DO I EXIST?

There are five key reasons why a person exists. Each of them will help on the road to discovering ones life purpose and bring about a fulfillment deep within their heart. It all begins with knowing Him. *"And this is life eternal, that they might know thee the only true God, and Jesus Christ, whom thou has sent" (John 17:3 KJV).* This is the master key to living a meaningful life in Christ Jesus. There is nothing more beautiful than beholding the wonder of His Person. There is nothing more amazing than gazing at the glory of God in the person of Jesus Christ. Hunger must come back to the church. Too many Christians have exchanged Him for religion, but in the end religion never satisfies. It is time to long and crave after His presence, to recognize how much He is needed. The Bible tells us to grow in grace and in the knowledge of the Lord Jesus Christ.

# REASON #1
# TO KNOW HIS NATURE AND HIS CHARACTER

The best way to know the Lord Jesus Christ is through His Word. When a Christian opens the Bible they should look for His character; they should search for what He is like and aim to get an understanding of His nature. To know Him, one must spend time in His Word. No matter how much a person claims to know God; they only know Him as much as they know His Word. Becoming like Christ should be the top priority of every Christian. The Bible says in Romans 8:29 that all have been predestined to be conformed into the image of his Son. So although Christians may have various assignments, the expectation of God for every child is to become like Christ, and they can only become like Christ as they discover who He is. There is no better place to begin this journey than the Word of God. When a person commits and gives themselves to the study and meditation of the Word, they are transformed by it (Proverb 4:20-22). It has the power to change a person from the inside out. Every Christian should let their motivation to read, study and meditate on God's Word be to become like Him in every way.

The Bible is a living book and full of power (Heb. 4:12), it is not simply read and agreed with. Yes, it is important to gain knowledge of the Word, but until knowledge is upgraded into understanding it simply remains in the mind. When knowledge has its roots established so deep in a person that it begins to govern their actions, knowledge has been upgraded to understanding. This is where many of God's children fall short and why their growth in Christ becomes stagnant. It is possible to know much of the Word without experiencing personal transformation. This is called the theory of the word or mental knowledge. It has to be converted into understanding in order to work. Understanding is when the Word governs ones way of life and shapes their character and conduct. When knowledge begins to work for a person, it is called understanding, and when understanding begins to yield dividends, it is known as wisdom.

Mixing the Word of God with faith is the key to entering understanding and wisdom (Hebrews 4:2). How does one mix the word with faith? There are three disciplines that help achieve this aim: (1) Confess the Word: confess who Christ is to you, who you are in Christ, what Christ has done for you, and who Christ is in you. This is to become a lifestyle (Isaiah 59:21). (2) Meditate on the Word: Give yourself to meditation (Timothy 4:15). It is through meditation that the Word establishes roots in ones heart and becomes a part of their DNA. It becomes engrafted and makes you a champion (Psalms 119:97-100). (3) Practice the Word: applying the Word and living it out in daily life is how to develop spiritual stamina that causes you to live victoriously in the affairs of life (Joshua 1:8). These three disciplines will for work any person, in any culture or any society and will cause them to take on the nature and character of Christ in reality.

## REASON #2
## TO KNOW HIS WAYS AND PRINCIPLES

Scripture shows that both Moses and Paul sought after the person of God and His ways. Even though both men experienced glorious encounters, mighty miracles, discovered deep revelations and had a global impact through their ministries, their legacy was found in their personal walk with God. They had an unceasing passion to know God intimately (Ex 33:13-19; Ps 103:7; Phil 3:8-11). This is a powerful example for the body of Christ today. The desire to know more of God should not only constantly grow, but it should exceed any and all other desires in this life. In Exodus 33 it says, *"Teach me your ways so that I may know you and continue in your favor."* The Hebrew word "yada" is used in the Old Testament and is translated in English as the word "know" or "knowledge." It has a much deeper meaning than the English word, and means to perceive, understand, to believe and conform, to see, experience, obey and to recognize. God wants every Christian to KNOW him in this fashion. When a person comes to Christ, He takes away the stony heart and gives them a heart of flesh, a heart that is able to know Him. God wants to reveal Himself to humanity and wants to be understood. He longs for the fellowship of His creation. Jeremiah 24:7 says, *"And I will give them an heart to know me, that I am the LORD: and they shall be my people, and I will be their God: for they shall return unto me with their whole heart."*

So it is important to discover who God is in the Word and to build every area of ones life on this foundation, meaning His values, His nature, and His principles. Dividing life into seven basic units can do this. Christians should examine each area and ensure they are established on the values found in God's Word. These areas are as follows:

1. Spiritual life
2. Relational life
3. Physical life
4. Mental life
5. Vocational life
6. Financial life
7. Life's purpose

Each part must be established firmly on the value system of the Word of God. Build your relationships, especially your marriage, on the principles of God's Word. This will result in establishing the character needed for a successful and lasting relationship. Apply the same principles to other areas and the result will be a successful life, because it will be built and established on the values of God (Matthew 7:24-26). Finally, link each area of life to a kingdom concept. The first six areas must connect to the seventh, which is one's life purpose, and every believer's life purpose should be to serve Jesus Christ and the cause of His kingdom. Understand that these are not seven different areas of life moving in seven different directions, but one life that is built upon pursuing God and His purposes. Christians must use all that they have and all that they are to serve the King and His kingdom.

# REASON #3
# TO BRING HIM PLEASURE

God takes pleasure in His children, but this concept is often difficult to wrap ones mind around. What is man? James 4 says, *"What is the nature of your life? You are [really] but a wisp of vapor (a puff of smoke, a mist) that is visible for a little while and then disappears [into thin air]*. Human life seems so small when compared to the eternal God, but the truth is that humanity brings pleasure to the Father's heart. This is why ones personal relationship with God must never be neglected or become casual. It shouldn't be cold, stale or mechanic, nor should it be formal or ritualistic. Walking with God should be vibrant, exciting, full of life and full of energy. All Christians should live life on earth in a way that brings so much joy and pleasure to the Father's heart. Listed below are two fundamental ways to make this happen.

The first way is by delighting in Him, *"And I was daily his delight, rejoicing always before Him" (Pr 8:30 KJV)*. Christianity is a relationship and a relationship without fellowship is like a marriage without romance. God is calling people to an intimate, beautiful and fulfilling relationship. Think about the very first time you fell in love with your spouse and how you couldn't wait to be in their presence. Think of how often you talked and how frequent they occupied your thoughts. You were determined to please this person in every way. You wanted them to know that they were the only one who had captivated your heart. You were careful with each other, never wanting to hurt or offend the other person. These are beautiful thoughts! Why is it then that many couples can't remain this way? Why do couples lose this fire after a while? Why do relationships become casual or maybe even boring? The answer is lack of connection, fellowship, intimacy and romance. And just like a natural relationship, these elements are needed in relation to God as well. God is not looking for formalities, but authentic, sincere, heartfelt love and since His love doesn't change, it is up to each person to do their part by delighting in Him.

The second way to please God is by keeping His Word. There is a power in Christianity known only to those who are doers of the Word. When believers become doers of God's Word, their authority in the spirit grows, God's presence in their lives becomes stronger, and their knowledge of Him becomes real. These are people who have experienced its effectiveness and know its capabilities. It touches the heart of God when His children lay aside their own reasoning and just do what His Word instructs them to do. It brings pleasure to God when they choose to honor Him by honoring His Word. WHY? It's because the only way for a person to prove their love for God is by obeying His Word.

> *"Jesus answered and said unto him, If a man love me, he will keep my words: and my Father will love him, and we will come unto him, and make our abode with him." (John 14:23 KJV)*

There is no substitute for a life of obedience - not prayer, fasting or service. Anyone in love with Christ will endeavor to please Him in all things and this is why Christians should grow in their understanding of His love (Eph 3:17-19). It is from this love that they are able to love Him back. The secret is to remain connected to the Vine and abide in Him. If this is ones primary concern, obedience will surely follow. True obedience always flows from a heart that knows the depth, the breath, the length, and the height of the love of Christ.

## REASON #4
## TO BRING GLORY TO GOD

*"I have glorified thee on earth"* (John 17:4 KJV). Every Christ-follower has a personal responsibility to search out ways to bring glory to God's name. This is called strategic thinking (Acts 10:19), and it begins with discovering the priorities that are dear to the heart of God. This will most assuredly be connected to the command of the Great Commission, or "the discipleship of nations." This is the heartbeat of God and it is wisdom to make the priority of the kingdom ones own priority. Discover what God is thinking and

translate His agendas into ones personal life. Why is this important? It is important because God only does through a person what He has already done in them. So, a course of action must be taken in line with God's leading. Decisions must be made, and then acted upon. Actions are what give wheels to dreams, but in order to be most effective, actions must turn into results. Results are what give wings to one's dreams. So how does one bring glory to God? By spreading the influence of Jesus and His kingdom in the earth. *"I have manifested thy name unto the men which thou gavest me out of this world"* (John 17:6 KJV).

Carrying out the will of God is what brings glory to God. That is why James 4:6 says that God resists the proud, but gives grace to the humble. When Christians are humble and fulfilling the plan of God, they willingly give all glory and honor to Him. This is why God gives more grace! The more God elevates them, the more glory He receives.

## REASON #5
## TO FINISH YOUR LIFE'S ASSIGNMENT ON EARTH

*"I have finished the work which thou gavest me to do"* (John 17:4 KJV). There is a beautiful work that every Christian was created to fulfill and it is the platform needed to spread the influence of God's kingdom. It begins by downloading the blueprint of one's calling and assignment. Believers must learn how to hear God's voice in their inner-man. God always speaks to the heart, but paints pictures of the spoken word in the mind (Heb 10:16). When God speaks, whether it is through His Word, His voice in the inner-man, dreams or visions, write it down so the specificity of the message will not be forgotten. Then begin to think and meditate on the message (Acts 10:19). Think of how to use it and apply it. The idea may require further development, such as formulating plans and strategies in order to produce maximum results. So, one must understand the specifics of his or her assignment in life, get educated, trained and acquire the necessary skills needed to carry out the assignment successfully. Remember that the vessel is equally as important as

the treasure within it, and every person's work flows out of the core of who they are. It is important to make sure one has the capacity to finish strong. This includes spiritual, mental, physical, financial and relational capacities. People need the heart and brainpower, as well as the habits and character for greatness. The work given by God is always related to a societal ill, that is, it is always directed to solving a problem. It is important not only to understand ones calling, but to complete it successfully, and receive the victor's crown.

## YOU ARE THE SALT OF THE EARTH

> *"Ye are the salt of earth; but if the salt have lost his savor, wherewith shall it be salted? It is thenceforth good for nothing, but to be cast out, and to be trodden underfoot of men." (Matthew 5:13 KJV)*

The church of the Lord Jesus Christ is the only hope for the world. This is why the church must maintain her saltiness, rise up and take responsibility for society. The universal church is the heartbeat of the world and every local church is the soul of their city. It is time to season the world and believe in the possibility for change that lies within the power of the church. The church, the mountain that is established above all other mountains, a place of elevation, the city of the living God, possesses the power to transform.

## CORNELIUS' EXAMPLE

> *"There was a certain man in Caesarea called Cornelius, a centurion of the band called the Italian band, a devout man, and one that feared God with all his house, which gave much alms to the people, and prayed to God always. He saw in a vision evidently about the ninth hour of the day an angel of God coming in to him, and saying unto him, Cornelius. And when he looked on him, he was afraid, and said, what is it, Lord? And he said unto him, Thy prayers and thine alms are come*

> up for a memorial before God. And now send men to Joppa, and call for one Simon, whose surname is Peter: He lodgeth with one Simon a tanner, whose house is by the sea side: he shall tell thee what thou oughtest to do." (Acts 10:1-6 KJV)

These scriptures reveal a powerful kingdom principle through the life of Cornelius. His example should be a reminder that nothing happens in the earth until someone takes responsibility. Think about it - an angel appeared to him, the Spirit of God was orchestrating the entire event, yet Cornelius' salvation was impossible without Peter. What is the principle? God always uses men to save men. God always uses people to save people. Peter was used as the salt of the earth to season and preserve the life of Cornelius. Every Christian still living on planet earth is the salt of the earth. Jesus said it and He was speaking to every man, woman and child.

You, the reader, are the very one the Lord is speaking to right now. Don't look to the person to your right or left; YOU are the salt of the earth. There lays within you the power to bring salvation and healing, to add flavor to those you come in contact with everyday. God wants you to begin now to take responsibility. You are the salt of the earth!

Salt is necessary to life. In fact, both humans and animals crave it. In human beings, it helps to maintain the delicate chemical balance of the body. Each cell in the human body is dependent on sodium; it is actually diffused throughout the fluid between cells. Each cell within the human body is like a small ocean containing salt water. It is no coincidence that salt is a white crystalline substance called sodium chloride. This color is also what represents the blood-washed ones.

> "Let us be glad and rejoice, and give honor to him: for the marriage of the lamb is come, and his wife hath made herself ready. And to her was granted that she should be arrayed in fine linen, clean and white: For the

fine linen is the righteousness of the saints." (Revelation 19:7-8 NLT)

The fact that God makes His children the salt of the earth is proof enough of the value they possess. There is something unique, special, and set apart about Christ-followers. They have meaning attached to their life and have something within to offer the world. As salt of the earth, Christians are a necessity to the world and required if transformation is to become a reality.

## THE PRINCIPLE OF RESPONSIBILITY

*And the word of the LORD came unto me, saying, Son of man, prophesy against the shepherds of Israel, Prophesy, and say unto them, Thus saith the Lord GOD unto the shepherds; Woe be to the shepherds of Israel that do feed themselves! Should not the shepherds feed the flocks? Ye eat the fat, and ye clothe you with the wool, ye kill them that are fed: but ye feed not the flock. The diseased have ye not strengthened, neither have ye healed that which was sick, neither have ye bound up that which was broken, neither have ye brought again that which was driven away, neither have ye sought that which was lost; but with force and with cruelty have ye ruled them. And they were scattered, because there is no shepherd: and they became meat to all the beasts of the field, when they were scattered. My sheep wandered through all the mountains, and upon every high hill: yea, my flock was scattered upon all the face of the earth, and none did search or seek after them. Therefore, ye shepherds, hear the word of the LORD; As I live, saith the Lord GOD, surely because my flock became a prey, and my flock became meat to every beast of the field, because there was no shepherd, neither did my shepherds search for my flock, but the shepherds fed themselves, and fed not my flock; Therefore, O ye shepherds, hear the word of the LORD;*

*Thus saith the Lord GOD; Behold, I am against the shepherds; and I will require my flock at their hand, and cause them to cease from feeding the flock; neither shall the shepherds feed themselves any more; for I will deliver my flock from their mouth, that they may not be meat for them. For thus saith the Lord GOD; Behold, I, even I, will both search my sheep, and seek them out. As a shepherd seeketh out his flock in the day that he is among his sheep that are scattered; so will I seek out my sheep, and will deliver them out of all places where they have been scattered in the cloudy and dark day. And I will bring them out from the people, and gather them from the countries, and will bring them to their own land, and feed them upon the mountains of Israel by the rivers, and in all the inhabited places of the country. I will feed them in a good pasture, and upon the high mountains of Israel shall their fold be: there shall they lie in a good fold, and in a fat pasture shall they feed upon the mountains of Israel. I will feed my flock, and I will cause them to lie down, saith the Lord GOD. I will seek that which was lost, and bring again that which was driven away, and will bind up that which was broken, and will strengthen that which was sick: but I will destroy the fat and the strong; I will feed them with judgment. And as for you, O my flock, thus saith the Lord GOD; Behold, I judge between cattle and cattle, between the rams and the he goats. Seemeth it a small thing unto you to have eaten up the good pasture, but ye must tread down with your feet the residue of your pastures? And to have drunk of the deep waters, but ye must foul the residue with your feet? And as for my flock, they eat that which ye have trodden with your feet; and they drink that which ye have fouled with your feet. Therefore thus saith the Lord GOD unto them; Behold, I, even I, will judge between the fat cattle and between the lean cattle. Because ye have thrust with side and with shoulder, and pushed all the diseased with your horns, till ye have scattered them abroad; therefore will I save my flock, and they shall no more be a prey; and I will judge between cattle and cattle. And I will set up one shepherd over them, and he shall feed them, even my servant David; he shall feed them, and he shall be their shepherd. And I the LORD will be their God, and my servant David a prince among them; I the LORD have spoken it. And I will make with them a covenant of peace, and will cause the evil beasts to cease out of the land: and they shall dwell safely in the wilderness, and sleep in the woods. And I will make them and the places round about my hill a blessing; and I will cause the shower to come down in his season; there shall be showers of blessing. And the tree of the field shall yield her fruit, and the earth shall yield her increase, and they shall be safe in their land, and shall know that I am the LORD, when I have broken the bands of their yoke, and delivered them out of the hand of those that served themselves of them. And they shall no more be a prey to the heathen, neither shall the beast of the land devour them; but they shall dwell safely, and none shall make them afraid. And I will raise up for them a plant of renown, and they shall be no more consumed with hunger in the land, neither bear the shame of the heathen any more. Thus shall they know that I the LORD their God am with them, and that they, even the house of Israel, are my people, saith the Lord GOD. And ye my flock, the flock of my pasture, are men, and I am your God, saith the Lord GOD." (Ezekiel 34:1-31 KJV)*

Every Christian is a shepherd. This term does not refer solely to the pastor of a local church, but to every member of the body of Christ. That is why they must be raised with this understanding. Ones workplace is not only a place where they can earn a living, it is also a parish, and they are the pastor. Their responsibility is to see their work as an expression of worship and to bring kingdom values into this environment. How? Through honesty, integrity, going above and beyond, being a peacemaker, etc. All of these values establish the kingdom of God as a means to bringing transformation. So according to the above chapter, God will hold all shepherds accountable. What is true for the shepherds in the local church is also true for the shepherds in the marketplace.

## FAITH FOR NATIONS

> *"Ask of me, and I shall give thee the heathen for thine inheritance, and the uttermost parts of the earth for thy possession." (Psalm 2:8 KJV)*

Most Christians are familiar with "faith" and they have been taught how to develop faith for healing, faith for provision, even faith for cars and houses and all kinds of "stuff." While not all of this is wrong, there is an overemphasis in teaching faith for material blessings that has left the church very inward focused and has given rise to a generation of self-centered people. *"For a man's life does not consist in the abundance of the things he possesses" (Luke 12:15).* All the blessings that come from God must be kingdom connected, meaning that all of life and all that consists of life here on earth are for Christ and for the cause of His kingdom. A true detachment from things is the only way to serve the purposes of God.

> *"Thine, O Lord, is the greatness, and the power, and the glory, and the victory, and the majesty: For all that is in the heaven and in the earth is thine; thine is the kingdom…" (I Chronicles 29:11 KJV)*

> *"…For all things come of thee, and of thine own have we given thee. For we are strangers before thee, and sojourners, as were all our fathers: our days on the earth are as a shadow, and there is none abiding. O LORD our God, all this store that we have prepared to build thee a house for thine holy name cometh of thine hand, and is ALL THINE OWN." (I Chronicles 29:14-16 KJV)*

It is extremely important to understand that everything related to life here on earth belongs to God - ones spouse, children, and possessions. The science of life validates this fact. It is no coincidence that mankind comes into this world naked and exits it the same way. All that is acquired between birth and death is simply entrusted, and will be accounted for. Those in the world, including some in the body of Christ, are under an illusion that they own their life and possessions and as a result live as they please. This is a lie of Satan (1John 5:19). Christians are called to transfer ownership of their lives to the Lordship of Jesus Christ. He alone must become the Lord of their lives, finances, home, family, business, time, abilities and resources. Paul called himself a prisoner of the Lord (Eph. 4:1).

> "And ye are not your own? For ye are bought with a price." (1 Corinthians 6:19-20 KJV)

It is only when Christ becomes the center of ones life that meaning and purpose are experienced. It is important for people to ask God to help them number their days (Ps 90:12) and to take on the attitude of Paul as "having nothing, and yet possessing all things" (2 Corinthians 6:10). Why not use faith to believe for the salvation of entire households, for communities, cities and nations? Christians must begin to develop faith that can bring transformation and change at every level of society.

## FUNCTIONS OF SALT IN THE HUMAN BODY

- Salt extracts excess acidity from cells in the body, particularly brain cells
- Salt generates hydroelectric energy in cells, which powers the energy needed by the cells
- Salt absorbs food particles through intestinal tract
- Salt stabilizes irregular heartbeats and is essential to regulate blood pressure in conjunction with water (the proportions are critical)
- Salt clears up catarrh and congestion of the sinuses
- Salt balances sugar levels in the blood

- Salt is needed for nerve cell communication and processing information with brain cells (from conception until death)
- Salt strengthens bones, as osteoporosis is a result of salt and water shortage in the body
- Salt prevents varicose and spider veins on the legs and thighs
- Salt is vital for sleep regulation (REF: DR. BATMANGHELIDJ'S BOOK, "WATER: RX FOR A HEALTHIER PAIN FREE LIFE.")

It is important to note that there is a very big difference between table salt and sea salt. Sea salt contains 84 mineral elements that the body needs and table salt is missing 81 of them. It is easy to see what Jesus meant when He said, "You are the salt of the earth." Christians bring health and are a basic necessity to life. Listed below are some of these minerals and their function in the body:

*Sodium*: Essential to digestion and metabolism, regulates body fluids, nerve and muscular functions

*Chlorine*: Essential component of human body fluids

Calcium: Needed for bone mineralization

*Magnesium*: Dissipates sodium excess, forms and hardens bones, ensures mental development, and sharpens intelligence, promotes assimilation of carbohydrates, retards the aging process and dissolves kidney stones

*Sulfur*: Controls energy transfer in tissue, bone and cartilage cells, essential for protein compounds

*Silicon*: Needed in carbon metabolism and for skin and hair balance

*Iodine*: Vital for energy production and mental development, ensures production of thyroid hormones, needed for strong auto-defense mechanism (lymphatic system)

*Bromine:* In magnesium bromide form, a nervous system regulator and restorer, vital for pituitary hormonal function

*Phosphorus:* Essential for biochemical synthesis and nerve cell functions related to the brain, constituent of phosphoproteins, nucleoproteins, and phospholipids

*Vanadium:* Of greater value for tooth bone calcification than fluorine, tones cardiac and nervous systems, regulates phospholipids in blood, reduces cholesterol (REF: ALTERNATIVE MEDICINE ANGEL)

These are just ten of the eighty-four minerals in sea-salt and it is already clear just how much the human body needs salt. Let this paint a picture of how much the world needs Christians as the salt of the earth.

## FUNCTIONS OF SALT

Although there are close to 14,000 functions of salt, most of these functions can be categorized into two main areas. The first is that salt acts as a preserving agent. As an anti-microbial control agent it suppresses the growth of spoilage organisms. It preserves meat and fish from decaying by controlling fermentation and by slowing down the decaying process.

## PRESERVING LIFE FROM DECAY

The primary function of the church as salt of the earth is to preserve life from corruption and decay. The church has within her the answer for societal ills such as systemic corruption and poverty. Dealing with these issues from the root requires strategies, wisdom and understanding of how to dismantle structures built upon worldly value-systems. Only after they are dismantled can Christians erect in its place structures built upon the value-systems of the kingdom of God.

*"… For God sent me ahead of you to preserve life" (Genesis 45:5 AMP).* Each person in the body of Christ exists to preserve life on earth. This is a mission that must be clearly seen so individuals can take responsibility. Christians are the salt of the earth; they are not churchgoers, benchwarmers or church workers. They are a treasure that is destined to serve humanity. It all begins with discovering purpose, and purpose is revealed by discovering Christ.

There is a vision God placed in you, even at birth, and it is vital that you discover it, excel in it and use it to serve Him by serving humanity. Joseph understood that God had raised and trained him for one purpose - to preserve the earth from death and decay. May you also discover your life's purpose in the kingdom of God.

## WHERE DO WE START?

To preserve lives, one must ask the question, "How are lives being destroyed?" It is being destroyed because of structures and systems built on the value-system of this world whose prince is Satan (1 John 5:19; Ephesians 2:2; 2 Corinthians 4:4). Many people are being raised in systems that do not have the values of God. This creates not only mindsets that are unwilling to submit to the Word of God, but also symptoms such as poverty, addiction, prostitution, abuse, divorce, etc. The church must train believers how to discover God's vision for their life. Pastor Sunday Adelaja says "The focal point of ones calling is where their pain and passion intersect." This means that a person can often discover their purpose in life by what bothers them the most, yet are passionate about changing. Pastors and other five-fold ministry gifts are to train, raise, and release people to fulfill these assignments that are outside the four walls of the church. Every Christian must begin the journey of self-discovery. The key is to discover Christ, and in discovering Him, one discovers their gifts and purpose in life. The more that one pursues Christ as their primary focus; layers will be unveiled and reveal his or her assignment in life. This communion is of vital importance, because it is impossible to do the work of God through human strength.

It is also important to excel in your field of endeavor. As a child of the king, choose to be the best in your field, as a means to establishing God's kingdom in this area. Training and education are vital to natural and spiritual success. Connect your assignment to one or more of the seven structures of society. For example, are you called to the business sector or educational sector? What areas within the educational system do you intend to change? Define it with the ultimate goal of displacing world systems with kingdom values. Plan, strategize, and get a working blueprint. It must go beyond the treatment of symptoms and cure root-causes. Find like-minded people who share the same passion and work together as a team.

It is also important to consciously pursue the character of the King. His character and values go hand in hand and cannot be divorced one from the other. Christians must continually grow and exemplify Christ-like qualities in their own lives. The world must see Jesus through His people. Christ is the example of how to walk with God, and how to display Him to the world. Christians must reflect His nature and display His glory if they want to make an impact in the world around them.

## TAKING RESPONSIBILITY AND PRESERVING LIVES

A very influential and wealthy woman traveled multiple times to an African nation. During each visit she became overwhelmed by the systemic poverty and corruption, especially when she saw the effect it had on the children. It literally broke her heart and she could not contain her tears. She instinctively knew she couldn't handle the problem single-handedly, so she thought of what she could do and how to take responsibility. This woman chose to focus on young girls and build an academy that would sponsor its students from high school all the way through college. This academy is one of the best in the nation and is transforming the lives of those attending the school. This individual saw a problem, took responsibility, and in doing so preserved lives.

## UNDERSTANDING A DIFFERENT DIMENSION OF THE HOLY SPIRIT

*"And the spirit of the LORD shall rest upon him, the spirit of wisdom and understanding, the spirit of counsel and might, the spirit of knowledge and of the fear of the LORD;" (Isaiah 11:2)*

Although the characteristic of the Holy Spirit that is most embraced by the church is the "Spirit of might", there are four out of seven characteristics that point to the operation of the mind. Within many charismatic movements there is an over-emphasis on emotional experiences, falling under the power, shaking and other bodily movements, but there is so much more to the Holy Spirit than this. In Exodus 35, verses 31-35, there is a different, more tangible manifestation of the Holy Spirit in constructing and rebuilding a nation. There is an anointing that manifests in creativity in providing tangible solutions of solving societal ills. It reveals itself in science, technology, medicine, construction, agriculture, and wealth creation. It deals with systemic root causes such as poverty and corruption. It produces divine blueprints, strategies, value-systems, structures, analysis, and operational systems to solving global problems and sustaining lasting prosperity. Bezaleel was filled with the Spirit of God in wisdom and understanding and in knowledge and all manner of workmanship. He was anointed with the ability to build the tabernacle of Moses. This is the anointing needed in the body of Christ today. This is the empowerment that can transform nations and use men and women of God to bring the values and principles of the kingdom of God.

## SALT FLAVORS FOOD

The second primary function of salt is to bring flavor (Job 6:6). It not only seasons food, but also suppresses other taste responses such as sweet, sour, and bitter. This salt additive has a functional factor in modifying food through a complex chemical reaction that provides a desirable finished product. Salt can give taste to a meal and makes it desirable, just as Christians can add meaning to people's lives by revealing what life is all about and how to live it abundantly.

## FLAVORING THE WORLD

Christians flavor the world through kingdom values. They season the world through the beatitudes of Christ, revealing His nature and attributes. The world is seasoned through God's love, His selflessness and compassion. He is on display 24/7 through his church. The more we conform to His image, the more power there is to show Him as He really is. This is not acting like Christ, or following rules or gaining head knowledge. It's in cooperation with the Holy Spirit that Christians truly become like Him and take on His nature. Looking like Christ is what happens when the Word of God is built and established in a person, through the Spirit of God. This is how the world is flavored, when Christ is revealed to, in and ultimately through the life of a believer.

## JESUS CHRIST IS GOD'S REVELATION TO THE WORLD

*"His son is the reflection of God's glory and the exact likeness of God's being."(Hebrews 1:3 GWT)*

Jesus Christ is an exact representation of God the Father. There is no one, past or present, who could even come close to revealing the Father. Jesus is God in human flesh (John 1:1-3, 14), and when a person sees Christ, he sees the Father (John 14:9). The ultimate goal of the Christian walk is to come to the knowledge of the Son of God, to mature into His likeness, and to come to the measure of the stature of the fullness of Christ as a means to transforming the world for Him (Ephesians 4:13). The bride of Christ, the church, must get a heart felt revelation that this is her primary responsibility and that to fulfill it, she must experientially put on Christ (Galatians 3:27).

## OBJECTIVE AND SUBJECTIVE TRUTH

Objective truth is truth that has been established because of what Christ did on behalf of His church. The mission that Jesus came to fulfill is a finished work, a complete work and cannot be improved upon. When a person is born of God, they become new creations in Christ. As a new creation, there are qualities and characteristics of God that are inherited, but they are in seed form (John 1:12-13; I John 3:9; 4:4,6; 5:4; 3:3,5,8). Read the following gifts that God imparts to His children at the new birth.

1. **The Life of God:** Every Christian has the life of God working on the inside of them. It is resident with them now, in the present. This life is what enables them to live like God in the earth. *"…He gave us the very life of Christ himself, the same new life with which, He quickened Him"* (Ephesians 2:5 AMP).
2. **The Love of God:** God's love is a perfect love and is placed in ones heart at salvation. God's love is a perfect love and it enables Christians to love others as He loves. *"… Because the Love of God is shed abroad in our hearts by the Holy Ghost, which is given unto us"* (Romans 5:5 KJV).
3. **The Grace of God**: The reason God has such a high standard for His church is because He has given them grace. Grace is divine enablement, divine ability, to accomplish what is not possible in human strength. *"And of His fullness have all we received, and grace for grace"* (John 1:16 KJV).
4. **The Holy Spirit of God:** The Spirit of God lives in the human spirit of every believer. He reveals Jesus and helps them conform to His image. *"What? Know ye not that your body is the temple of the Holy Ghost which is in you"* (I Corinthians 6:19 KJV).
5. **The Righteousness of God:** What allows God's children to freely live in His presence is righteousness. It is a gift that is given to Christians at salvation and enables them to approach God without fear. *"We are the righteousness of God in Christ Jesus."* (2 Corinthians 5:21 KJV)

6. **The Wisdom of God:** Wisdom is God's way of doing things and every believer has wisdom on the inside of them *"But of Him are ye in Christ Jesus, who of God is made unto us wisdom"* (I Corinthians 1:30 KJV).
7. **The Faith of God:** God has given believers a measure of His faith, which can be grown and developed to do mighty exploits. *"And Jesus, answering, said to them, have God's faith"* (Mark 11:22 BBE).
8. **The Mind of Christ:** Christians have the ability to think like Christ. *"But we have the mind of Christ"* (I Corinthians. 2:16 KJV).
9. **The Strength of God:** Children of God have access to His strength. Living in God's strength is a key to victorious living. *"To be strengthened and reinforced with mighty power in the inner man by the Holy Spirit Himself indwelling your innermost being"* (Ephesians 3:16 AMP).
10. **The Kingdom of God:** The Kingdom is within every believer. *"The Kingdom of God is within you* (Luke 17:21 KJV).
11. **The Anointing of God:** There is an anointing that abides in the children of God that equips them to do supernatural things for the glory of God *"But the anointing which ye have received of him abideth in you"* (I John 2:27 KJV).
12. **The Power of God:** God's power is at work in the believer. *"According to the power at work in us* (Ephesians 3:20 KJV).

The principle of the kingdom is that everything produces after its kind. Humanity was created in the image and likeness of God, and after being regenerated, they receive all of Him in seed form. Compare a seed being planted in the ground to the seed of God planted in the heart of man. The seed must be cultivated; the conditions for growth must be maintained. The light of the Word and the water of the Holy Spirit help the believer to grow and begin to see God reflected in his or her own life.

The challenge is that many of God's people believe and confess these truths without living them out in practice. Have you ever asked, "How can people hear God's Word for years, sit in church, yet have no visible change?" Well, there is objective truth in Scripture (positional) and subjective truth (experiential). For example, we are the righteousness of God in Christ (2 Cor. 5:21), we have the mind of Christ (1 Cor. 2:16), and we are dead to sin (Rom. 6:2). These beautiful truths are the foundation that every Christian should build upon, but it's not enough to have head knowledge. The Word cannot change a person if it only remains in the mind. All objective truth must become subjective to the believer. This is done on a personal level by cooperating with the Holy Spirit as he helps make positional truth ones personal reality. It is something that must be worked out *"...Workout (cultivate, carry out to the goal, and fully complete) your own salvation with reverence and awe and trembling)..." (Philippians 2:12 AMP)*

The objective truth is that as He is, so are Christians in this world (I John 4:17). God expects His children to reflect the nature and character of His Son, Jesus Christ, who is the one they confess to know and love. Most people do not have an issue with Jesus; but with how He is represented here on earth. It is easy for ones habits, conduct, lifestyle, and mindset to preach a contrary gospel. Every believer must sink into Christ until they are swallowed up by His life (Galatians 3:27). Just hearing God's Word and gaining knowledge only makes one more religious, but when the Holy Spirit deals with ones hearts, the life of God begins to take over and flow effortlessly from within. The Word of God is as deep as God. It is powerful and it is alive, and as it is planted in the heart of man, they become like Christ in reality.

## THE FUNDAMENTALS OF THE CHARACTER OF CHRIST

> *"Dear friends, let us continue to love one another, for love comes from God. Anyone who loves is a child of God and knows God. But anyone who does not love does not know God, for God is love. God showed us how much he loved us by sending his one and only Son into the world so that we might have eternal life through him. This is real love – not that we loved God,*

*but that he loved us and sent his Son as a sacrifice to take away our sins. Dear friends, since God loved us that much, we surely ought to love each other. No one has ever seen God. But if we love each other, God lives in us, and his love is brought to full expression in us." (1 John 4:7-12 NLT)*

LOVE: Love is the most powerful weapon in the world today. It is more than God's nature; it is God Himself. Nothing compares to the love of God and it is impossible to have this love without being born of God. Only those who have received it have the capacity to share it with others. God's love is the bedrock of Christianity and distinguishes it from other religions in the world. One of the main responsibilities Christians have is to develop their love walk from the beginning of their Christian faith. It is important to get ones roots established deep in Christ, and this happens by making a practice of walking in love. Nothing makes one more beautiful than the character of God's love. Putting on the love of God is putting on Christ. This is what character is all about. Love must be cultivated as a habit in order to be taken on as a reality. It will manifest Christ to a world that is so in need of love and will captivate the very hearts of His enemies. It will melt the hardest of heart and conquer the greatest foe.

SELFLESSNESS: *"There is no greater love than to lay down one's life for one's friends." (John 15:13 NLT)* Life is a privilege; it is a gift of trust, and it is best lived when understood. Because there is such a lack of knowledge and understanding, life is being abused all over the world. A true understanding of life's purpose will set people free from the demands and cares of this world. Life is about living for Christ and for the cause of His kingdom. When a person gains an understanding of this truth, it eradicates self-centeredness and futility of thinking. This is how Jesus lived. He lived for the Father and for humanity. God is the owner of life and humanity is the steward, responsible for it until called upon to give it back to its rightful owner (Ecclesiastes 8:8). The secret to a successful life in Christ is to relinquish ownership and take your rightful place as a steward. You must understand that life is only worth living when living for Christ and the cause of His kingdom. To live for Him, is to die for others. *"Because he hath poured out his soul unto death." (Isaiah 53:12 KJV)* Don't be afraid to lose your life for Him. Don't be afraid to give until there is nothing left to give. This is the way of the cross, the way of the kingdom and the way of Christ.

COMPASSION: *"But when he saw the multitudes, he was moved with compassion on them, because they fainted, and were scattered abroad, as sheep having no shepherd." (Matthew 9:36 KJV)* This characteristic of Christ is very profound. Jesus had eyes for people and He could see right into their souls. He saw their condition, their state and their need of a Savior. He saw how priceless and valuable each person was. He saw people and He knew they were His greatest treasure. To love God is to love people. Ones love towards God is proven in their ability to love others. Christians must take on the eyes of God in order to see as He sees. When people are seen through the eyes of God, hearts are moved with compassion. That movement is the emotion of the Holy Spirit flowing through the human heart for the condition of humanity. Compassion is more than feeling sorry or pity for someone. It is always accompanied by action (Luke 10:30-37). It is best expressed through acts of mercy and justice. Compassion seeks to take responsibility for humanity. It possesses a genuine interest in those to whom it is caring for. It seeks to bring restoration and wholeness and not simply relief. Moreover, compassion sees people for who they could be and not for who they presently are. It sees the best in the worst. The secret to the healing and miracle ministry of Jesus was compassion.

HUMILITY: *"Let this mind be in you, which was also in Christ Jesus: Who being in the form of God, thought it not robbery to be equal with God: But made himself of no reputation, and took upon him the form of a servant, and was made in the likeness of men: And being found in fashion as a man, he humbled himself, and became obedient unto death, even the death of the cross." (Philippians 2:5-8 KJV)* Jesus Christ represents the kingdom model for a life of excellence, and as seen in the above scripture, a perfect blueprint for a life of humility. The Lord Jesus, of His own free will, emptied Himself of all divine privileges and walked the earth as a servant. Taking on this virtue is imperative to displaying Christ to the world, and is an essential component of the character of the kingdom. This attitude should become the trademark of the church. Humility comes from understanding that we are who we are only by the grace of God. It is acknowledging God as the sole factor behind success in life. *"Paul may plant and Apollos may water, but it is God who gives the increase."* Humility should become evident, both internally and externally, and the secret to being filled with God's fullness is to be constantly emptied out of self. Jesus said, "I can of mine own self do nothing." Christians should endeavor to always make room for God's power to flow through them.

PURITY: *"But as he which hath called you is holy, so be ye holy in all manner of conversation."* Purity is a very strong and important virtue in the kingdom and God expects His children to conduct their entire pilgrimage on earth in a worthy manner. There are so many advantages to a living a holy life. For instance, it enables one to constantly enjoy the presence of God and to constantly hear from God. Sin is a hindrance that always gives the enemy a foothold in ones life. This can bring havoc and confusion in a Christian's life. The practice of sin veils the mind in darkness and weakens the strength of the inner-man. God made provision from the power of sin through the death and resurrection of Jesus Christ, and has given the ability to live and conduct ones life in holiness. Purity is not an option, but a command for citizens of the kingdom. Even so, God's indwelling presence will purify a believer from the inside out. The Holy Spirit is there to help assist believers and empower them to live a life of purity. Christians must be careful never to justify sin or to make light of it. Refuse to yield to, indulge in or intentionally be exposed to sin. It is important to build one's entire life according to the principles of God's Word and develop principles for living a holy life.

OBEDIENCE: *"And became obedient unto death, even the death of the cross."* Obedience to God is obedience to His Word. The Word of

God places so much emphasis on Christians leading an obedient life, and there is simply no substitute for it. Obedience to God must flow out of a heart filled with love for Him. Those who obey the Word are called "doers of the Word" or "practitioners of the Word." Christ-followers should start early in their journey to practice the Word. Just like anything else in life, people naturally become good at what they constantly give themselves to. Every Christian should focus on reading, studying, confessing, meditating and practicing the Word of God. This is how to build the Word into one's life, until it takes on the character of the Word. Practicing the Word will make it become flesh, which will give it material expression. Practitioners are the ones who get to know its power and efficacy. Being obedient, or practicing the Word causes a person to develop deep roots in the knowledge of Jesus Christ, and the deeper the roots, the stronger the foundation. It is through obedience that a life is built on the rock (Luke 6:46-48), and is able to be stable in the tests and trials of life.

WISDOM: *"Whence hath this man this wisdom and these mighty works?"(Matthew 13:54 KJV)* Wisdom is the principle thing, meaning wisdom is the main thing, the essential thing and the most important virtue in commanding a life of success (Proverbs 4:7). Wisdom turns a person into a "master-strategist" in life. It makes him a master over the elements of this world's system. Wisdom is the key to living a life of victory and accomplishment. This is how it works. Knowledge is the accumulation of raw data. It may give light but not life. Knowledge in the realm of the mind cannot transform a person until it is converted into understanding. Understanding is when ones knowledge of a thing takes on material expression. That is, when it shapes one's character and governs their life. Wisdom, however, is when ones understanding yield dividends for him. It is when knowledge begins to bear fruit or results. A life without the wisdom of God is bankrupt, as it relies solely on human reasoning. Since wisdom is God's way of doing things, it gives access into the mindset of God that equips a person to make a way out of no way.

All of these virtues were found in Christ and they are necessary to living the life of the kingdom. It is up to every believer to grasp hold of them, practice and make them flesh. Mental knowledge of them will not accomplish much; it is understanding that will cause them to take on material expression. Remember, the life in the Vine is of no value if it doesn't express itself in tangible fruit. Likewise, Christianity without Christ-likeness is the most dangerous threat to Christianity itself. It is an obstacle to the works and gospel of Christ Himself. It is through His character that the world can ultimately see Him and understand Him. It is through His Character that Christ is revealed and made known to a lost world. He shines through His church when she takes on the virtues of the kingdom, because the virtues of the kingdom are the virtues of Christ Himself. Christ-likeness, therefore, must become a priority in today's church as well as a priority in transforming the nations of the world.

## HOW TO TAKE ON THE CHARACTER OF CHRIST

- Set clearly defined goals, i.e. list areas of life that need change

- Customize a schedule for success

- Commit yourself through determination and discipline

- Translate your training into a lifestyle

- Don't stop until the Word is made flesh

    *"Ye are the salt of the earth: but if the salt have lost his savor wherewith shall it be salted? It is thenceforth good for nothing, but to be case out, and to be trodden under foot of men." (Matt. 5:13 KJV)*

# Chapter 4
# HINDRANCES TO A SALTED LIFE
## "KINGDOM CHARACTER AND KINGDOM VALUES"

*"Value-systems without Christ are not only unattainable but impossible" - Sino Agueze*

The process of losing a nation begins when people of God are being overridden by the culture and its values (Judges 3:5-16). Christians will always live in the world, but there should be a clear distinction between their values and those in the world. When the dividing line is no longer clear, there is then a need for a deliverer. When the values of people fade, and they begin to take on the values of the world, the fall of that nation has begun. People are what determine the greatness of a nation as well as the demise (I Sam 24:5-6).

> *"Righteousness exalteth a nation: but sin is a reproach to any people." (Proverbs 14:34 KJV)*

> *"Righteousness makes a nation great but sin degrades any people." (Proverbs 14:34 CJB)*

It has already been established that human nature is inherently corrupt in root and in branch, and without a re-creation of the human spirit; it is impossible to build and sustain a righteous nation. Only that which is born of God will manifest the values needed to sustain the greatness of a society. The best of morals without Christ as the center is totally bankrupt and void of the power to provide meaningful change. Creation fell into darkness the moment sin was introduced into the earth's sphere (Romans 5:12) and it is waiting for deliverance out of corruption into the glorious liberty of the sons of God; hence she groans in pain.

> *"For all creation is waiting patiently and hopefully for that future day when God will resurrect his children. For on that day thorn and thistles, sin death and decay- things that overcome the world against its will at God's command- will all disappear, and the world around us will share in the glorious freedom from sin which God's children enjoy." (Romans 8:19-21 TLB)*

Those who don't know Christ truly underestimate the fallen nature of the old Adamic life and its impact on creation. And those who do know Him must understand the work of the cross in dealing with the impact of the serpent's poison in man's tri-partite nature. Christians' must pursue the goal of becoming Christ-like in practice, in order to maintain their relevance as the salt of the earth (Romans 6:6, Ephesians 4:22-24).

## UNDERSTANDING THE SALTED LIFE

> *"You are like salt for the whole human race. But if salt loses its saltiness, there is no way to make it salty again. It has become worthless, so it is thrown out and people trample on it." (Matthew 5:13 GNT)*

Did you know that Jesus used this statement in 3 different incidents, at 3 different places, at 3 different times, to 3 different audiences? This statement ties into the 3 hindrances to living a salted life. The first hindrance is the self-life, which is found in the Gospel of Luke 14. This is the most dangerous impediment to the work of the Holy Spirit in a person's heart and to living a fruitful life. The second hindrance is found in the Gospel of Matthew 5, popularly known as "The Beatitudes of Christ," and is considered till date the greatest message rendered to man. The "Beatitudes" reveal saltiness in the world, without which, Christians cease to be useful to the kingdom of God. The third hindrance is found in the Gospel of Mark 9, and is known as "self-sabotage character traits." These traits identify those who betray Christ by their lifestyle.

## HINDRANCE ONE
## "THE SELF-LIFE"

> *"Large crowds were travelling with Jesus, and turning to them he said: If anyone comes to me and does not hate his father and mother, his wife and children, his brothers and sisters— yes, even his own life— he cannot be my disciple. And anyone who does not carry his cross and follow me cannot be my disciple. Suppose one of you wants to build a tower. Will he not first sit down and estimate the cost to see if he has enough money to complete it? For if he lays the foundation and is not able to finish it, everyone who sees it will ridicule him, saying, 'This fellow began to build and was not able to finish.' Or suppose a king is about to go to war against another king. Will he not first sit down and consider whether he is able with ten thousand men to oppose the one coming against him with twenty thousand? If he is not able, he will send a delegation while the other is still a long way off and will ask for terms of peace. In the same way, any of you who does not give up everything he has cannot be my disciple. Salt is good, but if it loses its saltiness, how can it be made salty again? It is fit neither for the soil nor for the manure heap; it is thrown out. He who has ears to hear, let him hear." (Luke 14:25-35 KJV)*

The self-life is the greatest hindrance to a living a salted life. It originated with Satan and was proven during his rebellion against God (Isa. 14:12-14). Self distorts the mind and ones spiritual sight; how else could Satan literally believe He could fight against God and win? This rebellion is what led to self-government apart from God. *"These be they… sensual, having not the Spirit." (Jude 1:19 KJV)* In the first Adam, every person died and inherited a self-induced nature (1 Cor. 15:22). Think about sin, irrespective of the type; it is all rooted in the desire to please self. This is the type of nature mankind was born with, and this is the nature that still attempts to rise and take over. Since the beginning of time, creation has fought against the rule of God "...*We will not have this man to reign over us*" (Luke 19:14 KJV).

Let's take a look at the make-up of mankind. Man is essentially a spirit (1 Thess. 5:23; Heb. 4:12; 2 Cor. 4:16; Rom. 7:22; 1 Pet. 3:4; Zech. 12:1; Job 10:11), has a soul (the mind, emotions and will), and lives in a physical body (2 Cor. 5:1-2 TLB). It was through Adam that the death of the human spirit occurred (Gen. 2:17). When Adam was disconnected from God through sin, he had no source other than himself and, as a result, the soul was enthroned (Gen 3:5). Originally the soul (the mind, emotions, and will) was designed to be a vessel of the human spirit, the ability to express to the world the workings of God in one's inner-man. When the soul was enthroned, it was no longer subservient to the spirit, but in fact, ruled over it. So as people live and grow and correspond with the world (Jam 4:4), the soul becomes filled with the love and spirit of this world (1Cor 2:12). Scripture defines the love of this world as the "lust of the flesh, the "lust of the eyes" and the "pride of life" (1 John 2:16).

> *"And they said, Go to, let us (self), build us (self) a city and a tower whose top may reach unto heaven; and let us (self), make us (self) a name..." (Genesis 11:4 KJV) {Emphasis mine}*

This is why "lust" (the love to sin) is the very foundation of the self-life. The "lust of the flesh" is centered in the soul, and is expressed as "works of the flesh" in the body (Gal. 5:19-21). By this fact alone, it is easy to see that the self-life is the stronghold of sin. To destroy the power of sin, one must destroy the root, the power of self.

You might be thinking - Is this even possible? Can I really deal with self? Where do I begin? How do I know if I am actually changing? The good news is that it is very possible. With an understanding of the Word of God and a willingness to rely on the finished work of Christ, every Christian can begin to live a victorious life out of the overflow of their spirit man. It is possible to live life under the government of God rather than the government of self.

Pray this prayer: *"Jesus - I believe that your Word is true and that you made a way for me to live a surrendered life. I ask right now that you open my eyes and ears to understand Your Word, to retain it, and to be changed by it. Holy Spirit, I invite you to teach me and guide me into this understanding. I declare that you are my source and I choose to rest in you. In Jesus name, amen."*

It is easy to think that becoming a new creation is the ultimate goal, but it is actually the beginning of a lifetime commitment that takes work, perseverance and endurance to complete. When a person puts their faith in Christ Jesus, he must allow the Word of the cross to divide soul from spirit (Heb 4:12). This is what allows our born-again spirit to be joined to the Spirit of the Lord (1Cor 6:17). Remember, before a person invites God to live in their heart, their soul and spirit were mingled and filled with the world. This division between the two is very important, because the poison of Satan that was released (Num. 21:6-9), affected every part of mankind, and as a result, requires sanctification (1 Thess. 5:23).

The Word of God, as the sword of the Spirit, was designed to reach the point where soul and spirit meet (as foreshadowed in the Old Testament). The priest flays open the sacrifice and cuts off all "fats" covering the inward parts (Lev. 3:3; 4:8). In the same way, the high priest of the New Testament must remove all influences of the old life in the soul (Rom. 7:5; 8:6-8) and the body (Rom. 7:21-23). Jesus regenerates the spirit, but Christians are responsible for renewing their minds and submitting their bodies as living sacrifices to God.

As stated in the beginning, the self-life hinders the spirit-life. Think about a seed and how its outer shell keeps the life of the seed locked within. It is when the seed dies, and the outer shell decays, that the life within breaks forth (Jn. 12:24). This life of the Holy Spirit was designed to flow from our born again spirit, bursting forth as rivers of living water, through the vessel of a sanctified soul, so that it is Christ living through the believer and accomplishing the will of God in the earth.

Even while reading this, look to the finished work of the cross (Zech. 12:10) and see you baptized into His death (Rom. 6:3-4). It is in Christ's death that we are dead to sin and disconnected from its power (Rom. 6:7-9). It is in His death that we can declare by faith that we are indeed dead to sin (Rom. 6:11), refuse to let sin reign in our mortal bodies, and choose to live unto God as those raised out of the power of sin and death (Rom. 6:12).

## BEWARE OF DOUBLE STANDARDS

Most Christians are familiar with obvious outward "sins," which are known as the "works of the flesh" (Gal. 5:19-21). These are easy to see and easy to judge, however it's the more subtle forms of the self-life that can evade detection. People naturally tend to major on the "fruits of sin" and minor on the "root of sin." However, they both have equal power to affect the saltiness of a Christian's life and their ability to season the world.

The Lord Jesus in the gospels lifted the veil over the self-life. He mentions family (Matt. 10:37-39), self-preservation (Matt. 16:21-25); earthly things (Luke 17:32-33); and He climaxed it with self-love (John 12:25). All of these can hinder and quench the life in the spirit. This soulish life is the life Christians must lose in order to gain the higher life. It is easy for the body of Christ to work hard at treating the symptoms of self, but it takes a power greater than any human effort to cure the root. Think of how many formulas and worldly methods are used to try and make people feel good, have self-esteem or have a sense of value. Human effort penetrates no further than the soul, and only patches up the wounds of the "works of the self-life," leaving the root of the self-life firmly in place.

Think about the words of Paul *"For, to me to live is Christ…"* This is a question that every Christian should ask, "Is Christ a part of my life or is He my all in all? Do I love Him more than the things mentioned above? Is Christ what gives meaning and purpose to my life? If the answer is YES, then, is the proof of your discipleship evident? Do you daily carry the cross in relation to all things of this world and the spirit that governs it? Do you have prayer power? Is heaven's agenda your primary concern? It is time for the body of Christ to come back to prayer and spiritual strength. Satan has whispered lies and convinced so many that they are okay (especially in the western church). People think that identifying with a set of Christian beliefs, going to church or being a "good person" is enough, when there is actually no substitution for the proof of a transformed life. Christians are called to be the salt, called to be the light, called to be a city set on a hill that reflects the nature of Jesus Christ. Christian heritage can easily be used as a camouflage, but anything that takes His place, be it family, earthly things, pride or self-centeredness, in all its forms and shades, is idolatry.

## THE SELF-LIFE, THE SEED-LIFE, AND THE SALT-LIFE

*"He that loveth his life (psuche, self-life), shall lose it; and he that hateth his life (psuche, self-life) in this world shall keep it unto life eternal (Zoë, God-life)." (John 12:25 KJV emphasis mine)*

*"Verily, verily, I say unto you, except a corn of wheat fall into the ground and die, it abideth alone, but if it dies, it bringeth forth much fruit." (John 12:24 KJV)*

*"And he said, bring me a new cruse, and put salt therein… And he went forth unto the spring of the waters, and cast the salt in there and said, thus saith the Lord, I have healed these waters; there shall not be from thence any more death or barren land." (2 Kings 2:20-21 KJV)*

It is important to analyze how salt works, so believers can use it to measure their own life. A tincture of salt can perfectly season a pot of soup, and the effect occurs in the solution. Think about the last time you used salt to season your food. Unlike pepper, it is no longer visible to the eye once it has been poured out. This can be compared to a type of death - it completely dissolves, loses its outward texture, yet releases its power, which changes the overall flavor of the soup.

Ezekiel, the forty-seventh chapter, speaks of this life as torrents of living water flowing from the throne-room of God into the Dead Sea. Upon contact with the sea, it destroyed death by bringing life. In the New Testament, the river of God flows from ones spirit-man through the indwelling of the Holy Spirit. If the soul is filled with self, it imprisons the life of God. Only as believers die daily can the life of God be released from within.

> *"Always bearing about in the body the dying of the Lord Jesus that the life also of Jesus might be made manifest in our body. For we which live are always delivered unto death for Jesus' sake, that the life also of Jesus might be made manifest in our mortal flesh. So then death worketh in us, but life in you." (2 Corinthians 4:10-12 KJV)*

This is what the world needs today. The whole earth is groaning, and in pain, needing deliverance from the bondage of sin and death. There are people who are depending on you to be the salt that preserves and seasons their life. It is in giving ones life to God that much fruit is produced from a single seed.

> *"I assure you, most solemnly I tell you, unless a grain of wheat falls into the earth and dies, it remains [just one grain; it never becomes more but lives] by itself alone. But if it dies, it produces many others and yields a rich harvest." (John 12:24 AMP)*

## HINDRANCE TWO
## "THE BEATITUDES"

The second hindrance to the salted life is lack of the beatitudes being present in believers' lives. The beatitudes are BE-attitudes, they are not laws to be followed or commandments to be adhered to, but rather attitudes that believers must cultivate and make their own. The beatitudes are so beautiful because they reflect the heart of Jesus Christ. They are the values and character of the kingdom of God. As citizens of this kingdom, we are to take hold of these values in order to become ambassadors and properly represent the King. When believers cultivate these values, they are able to season the world around them and shine forth the beauty of Christ to those blinded by the darkness (2 Co 4:4). Without them, the church loses her relevance, influence and power in the earth.

## BEATITUDE ONE

> *"Blessed are the poor in spirit: for theirs is the kingdom of heaven." (Matthew 5:3 KJV)*

> *"Spiritually prosperous are the destitute and helpless in the realm of the spirit, because theirs is the kingdom of heaven." (Mathew 5:3 Went)*

The first beatitude says blessed are the poor in spirit, for theirs is the kingdom of heaven. Jesus was not talking about financial poverty, because someone who is poor can be just as mean, in sin and ungodly as anyone else. The meaning of this word "poor" in the Greek means one who has nothing and is completely empty. It means abject poverty; utter helplessness; complete destitution; subsisting on the alms of others. It paints the picture of the beggar at the beautiful gate, crippled from birth and needing assistance just to survive (Acts 3:2).

The poor in spirit are those who understand that they are nothing apart from God. The world teaches us, in a very subtle way, that our value and worth are found in things outside of ourselves: what type of family we come from, our education, our physical appearance, our career, our wealth, etc. There is nothing wrong with these things, but if they are the source of our value and worth, we are in trouble. There is always someone who is more attractive, smarter, in a higher position, more educated, or wealthier, and these things can be taken away in a moment.

Christians must recognize and embrace this poverty of spirit. Even Jesus, who was anointed without measure said, "The son can do nothing of himself" (John 5:19); "I can of mine own self do nothing" (John 5:30); "My doctrine is not mine, but his that sent me" (John 7:16); "For I have not spoken of myself" (John 12:49)." Jesus repeatedly acknowledged that he was fully dependent on the Father and not on Himself. Anything that is sourced in self leaves God out of the equation. It has no carrying power in the kingdom of God because it is concerned with its own interest, not that of the Father's.

An example of someone who was poor in spirit is the prodigal son (Luke 15:11-32). Here is this young man, who left his father's house in pride and arrogance, wasted his inheritance in a far away country. There was a severe famine; he had no job and nothing to eat. At that point, the Bible says, he came to himself; he sobered up, and the reality of his condition was made plain to him. He returns to his father and said, *"I have sinned against heaven and against you. I am no longer worthy to be called your son" (Luke 15:21)*. This is being poor in spirit. He was completely empty both physically and spiritually, and knew that He was nothing apart from His father, who in this parable represents Father God. He was humbled by the reality of his current state. It takes humility to be poor in spirit. In fact, the more a person grows in Christ the more they realize their need of Him.

When Christians take on the attitude of being poor in spirit, they are able to see their spiritual condition as well as the greatness of their God. The stark contrast between the two causes them to fall to their knees, humble themselves, and cry out to the living God. The Word of God says that the heart is desperately wicked (Jer. 17:9).

There is no way for mankind to fully understand the depth of the human heart and what lies in it. When Christians understand they are nothing apart from God, it results in their understanding of their great need of God. They are not deceived or foolish enough to believe they can make it on their own, apart from their creator. It is in Him that we live, move and have our being, and that without Him we can do nothing (Acts 17:28; John 15:5).

It is time for the body of Christ to come under the full leadership of the Spirit of God and be governed by the Word of God. Every believer has been bought with a price and belongs to God, but He wants them to willingly depend on Him and lay down their lives in order to carry out His will in the earth. This dependence will produce in us Christ-like characteristics, and reveal the rule of Christ in our lives.

> *"You're blessed when you're at the end of your rope; with less of you, there is more of God and His rule."*
> *(Matthew 5:3 Message)*

There is a kingdom principle on dying to live; losing to gain; giving to get; humbling to exalt; becoming the least to become the greatest and decreasing to increase. The more one loses himself; the more of Christ the world can see.

> *"He that loveth his life - (psuche) shall lose it; and he that hateth his life - (psuche) in this world shall keep it unto life eternal - (Zoë)." (John 12:25 KJV) {Emphases mine}*

It's simple: the more of the self-life lost; the more of the God-life gained. To be swallowed up in His life (Col 3:3) is what causes the life of God to burst forth as rivers of living waters from within. The reign of Christ is first established in the heart and dependency on Him will cultivate the value of being poor in spirit.

Prayer: *God I acknowledge that I am in desperate need you and that I am nothing apart from you. Just as Christ could do nothing of Himself, I also can do nothing of myself. Today I commit once again to your Lordship and I ask you to reign in my heart and my mind. I lay down my life and ask you to use it to bring glory and honor to your name and to show the world who you really are. Amen.*

## BEATITUDE TWO

*"Blessed are they that mourn: for they shall be comforted." (Matthew 5:4 KJV)*

The second beatitude is one that is very noble and possessed only by a few. It is a rare virtue in today's world. Those who mourn in this beatitude are not mourning from a natural standpoint, i.e. mourning as an emotional response to loss or death. The mourning Jesus is talking about is a spiritual mourning over spiritual matters. It flows from the previous beatitude, blessed are the poor in spirit. When Christians realize their spiritual need and poverty, when they examine themselves in the light of God's Word and God's standard – they mourn.

People can mourn over their own lives, mourn over the lives of others who fail or fall short, mourn over the church when abuse of the grace of God is evident, etc. Jesus wept over Israel when she rejected God and killed her prophets. Even today it is possible to believe He still weeps over the state of the church, with so many people living beneath their rights and privileges in Christ. One can spiritually mourn over the world, when they see how many people are in bondage, in addiction and seem to have no hope. The psalmist himself mourned over the sins of God's people *"Tears stream down from my eyes, because they do not keep your law"* (Psalms 119:136 KJV).

Those who mourn do not rejoice at the fall or mishaps of others. They wail at the sinful state of a nation and its damaging effects on its people, resources and the land. It is with righteous grief they cry out in intercession for God's mercy to prevail over judgment (II Cor. 12:21). These are people who have great faith in God and wholeheartedly believe that their persistence in prayer will procure God's intervention in the lives and circumstances of a people.

## DAVID'S EXAMPLE

> *"And they mourned, and wept, and fasted until even, for Saul, and for Jonathan his son, and for the people of the LORD, and for the house of Israel; because they were fallen by the sword." (II Samuel 1:12 KJV)*

King Saul made a living out of trying to make David's life a living hell. He attempted three separate times to murder him. In short, Saul was David's archenemy who pursued him with one objective in mind - to destroy him from the face of the earth. It is no wonder that David was called a man after God's heart. Look at how David mourned for Saul and spoke so highly and kindly of him as he wept bitterly for the death of Saul.

> *"And David lamented with this lamentation over Saul and over Jonathan his son: (Also he bade them teach the children of Judah the use of the bow: behold, it is written in the book of Jasher.) The beauty of Israel is slain upon thy high places: how are the mighty fallen! Tell it not in Gath, publish it not in the streets of Askelon; lest the daughters of the Philistines rejoice, lest the daughters of the uncircumcised triumph. Ye mountains of Gilboa, let there be no dew, neither let there be rain, upon you, nor fields of offerings: for there the shield of the mighty is vilely cast away, the shield of Saul, as though he had not been anointed with oil. From the blood of the slain, from the fat of the mighty, the bow of Jonathan turned not back, and the sword of Saul returned not empty. Saul and Jonathan were lovely and pleasant in their lives, and in their death they were not divided: they were swifter than eagles, they were stronger than lions.*

> *Ye daughters of Israel, weep over Saul, who clothed you in scarlet, with other delights, who put on ornaments of gold upon your apparel. How are the mighty fallen in the midst of the battle! O Jonathan, thou wast slain in thine high places. I am distressed for thee, my brother Jonathan: very pleasant hast thou been unto me: thy love to me was wonderful, passing the love of women. How are the mighty fallen, and the weapons of war perished!"* (II Samuel 1:17-27 KJV)

Those who mourn, even for their enemies, are truly Christ-like in nature. How does one sing his enemy's praise like David? How is it that not one negative word came out of David's mouth? It was part of his gracious attitude (II Sam. 4:1-12). The body of Christ should never hand their brethren to the enemy and hang them out to dry like the Israelites handed out Samson to the Philistines (Jud. 15:11-13). They should pour out their hearts to God and intercede for mercy and restoration, mourning for those who fail. Christians should also be concerned about the spiritual, moral and material state of a people.

> *"And when he was come near, he beheld the city, and wept over it, Saying, If thou hadst known, even thou, at least in this thy day, the things which belong unto thy peace! But now they are hid from thine eyes. For the days shall come upon thee, that thine enemies shall cast a trench about thee, and compass thee round, and keep thee in on every side, And shall lay thee even with the ground, and thy children within thee; and they shall not leave in thee one stone upon another; because thou knewest not the time of thy visitation"* (Luke 19:41-44 KJV).

Jesus mourned for the blindness of Israel in not recognizing her true messiah and for the consequences that would befall them as a result of their blindness. Those who mourn will see the fruit of their labor, receive amazing answers to prayer and experience the joy of seeing lives changed and cities transformed by the power of God. Mourning produces within a believer God-like qualities that are priceless, beautiful and cannot be wrought in them any other way.

> *"For Godly grief and the pain God is permitted to direct, produce a repentance that leads and contributes to salvation and deliverance from evil, and it never brings regret; but worldly grief (the hopeless sorrow that is characteristic of the pagan world) is deadly (breeding and ending in death). For (you can look back now and) observe what this same godly sorrow has done for you and has produced in you: What eagerness and earnest care to explain and clear yourselves [of all complicity in the condoning of incest], what indignation [at the sin], what alarm, what yearning, what zeal [to do justice to all concerned]. What readiness to mete out punishment [to the offender]! At every point you have proved yourselves cleared and guiltless in the matter."*
> (II Corinthians 7:10-11 AMP)

Truthfully, people become more like Christ when they mourn for the conditions of the hearts of men, especially those who have been drawn away from God. These mourners understand the misery of sin, not only its consequences on human life, but more importantly, how it breaks the heart of God. There is a comfort that comes to those who mourn. *"Blessed is the man unto whom the LORD imputeth not iniquity, and in whose spirit there is no guile"* (Psalms 32:2).

## BEATITUDE THREE

> *"Blessed are the meek: for they shall inherit the earth."* (Matthew 5:5 KJV)

It is easy to misunderstand the word meekness. Many people equate meekness with weakness. They think if you are meek, you allow everyone to walk over you, that you are timid or passive. What does it really mean to be meek? The Greek word for meek was used to refer to trained animals, i.e. a strong and powerful horse that has been trained and disciplined so a human can control it. Meekness is great power under control, strength under control. The word meek used in Matthew 5:5 refers to a God controlled person; a man or woman whose strength is controlled by God, in thought, word, and deed. A person who is meek is trained and allows himself to submit to the will of God.

The scriptures give many examples of people who were meek, yet strong, at the same time. The first example is Moses, who was known as a great leader. He stood up to the most powerful leader in the world and led God's people through the wilderness to the border of the promise land. *"Now the man Moses was very meek, above all the men which were upon the face of the earth"* (Num. 12:3). So, the one who was meekest accomplished that which was greatest. Meekness allows Christians to draw from a source greater than themselves. Supernatural strength to accomplish the supernatural will of God. Think about Jesus, who could heal the sick and perform astonishing miracles. He spoke to the wind and to the waves and even brought the dead back to life. He said, *"Take my yoke upon you, and learn of me; for I am meek and lowly in heart: and ye shall find rest unto your souls" (Matt 11:29 KJV)*. Jesus was filled with meekness and lowliness of heart, yet accomplished the greatest mission of reconciling man back to God.

Meekness is the attitude that recognizes God as the true source behind success and greatness in life.

> *"Now therefore thus shalt thou say unto my servant David, Thus saith the LORD of hosts, I took thee from the sheepcote, even from following the sheep, that thou shouldest be ruler over my people Israel: And I have been with thee whithersoever thou hast walked, and have cut off all thine enemies from before thee, and have made thee a name like the name of the great men that are in the earth"(I Chronicles 17:7-8 KJV)*

Look at how God picked up David from being a shepherd boy to being king over Israel. The Lord gave him both success and victory over his enemies and gave David a great name among kings. All of this success was a result of God's presence with David, *"And I have been with thee whithersoever thou hast walked."* The meek, like Paul the Apostle often say, *"Who then is Paul, and who is Apollos, but ministers by whom ye believed, even as the Lord gave to every man I have planted, Apollos watered; but God gave the increase. So then neither is he that planteth any thing, neither he that watereth; but God that giveth the increase." (I Corinthians 3:5-7 KJV)*

The meek recognize God as the factor behind their success. The difference between the meek and the humble is that the meek have already attained some type of notoriety. They have influence, success and power, but are internally detached from it because they know it is sourced in God.

> *"But by the grace of God I am what I am: and his grace which was bestowed upon me was not in vain; but I labored more abundantly than they all: yet not I, but the grace of God which was with me."(I Corinthians 15:10 KJV)*

People who are meek do not have pride, self-conceit, an inflated ego or an attachment to self-importance. They do not see themselves more highly than they ought, nor do they walk around with a superiority complex. They are humble, submissive, and able to be corrected, teachable, gentle, modest, and full of mercy & compassion. They welcome all as equals and treat others, as they would have others treat them.

## CHARACTERISTICS OF MEEKNESS

### I. They are spiritual, yet sober-minded

> *"Brethren, if a man be overtaken in a fault, ye which are spiritual, restore such an one in the spirit of meekness;*

*considering thyself, lest thou also be tempted."*
*(Galatians 6:1 KJV)*

The meek possess strong values, integrity and fortitude. They have high moral standards, live by principle and have cultivated strong disciplines over the years. They are not naïve by thinking they have arrived, and understand that no one is immune from potential shortcomings.

## II. They are full of mercy and pray for those who falsely accuse them

> *"And Miriam and Aaron spake against Moses because of the Ethiopian woman whom he had married: for he had married an Ethiopian woman. And they said, Hath the LORD indeed spoken only by Moses? hath he not spoken also by us? And the LORD heard it. (Now the man Moses was very meek, above all the men, which were upon the face of the earth. And the LORD spake suddenly unto Moses, and unto Aaron, and unto Miriam, Come out ye three unto the tabernacle of the congregation. And they three came out. And the LORD came down in the pillar of the cloud, and stood in the door of the tabernacle, and called Aaron and Miriam: and they both came forth. And he said, Hear now my words: If there be a prophet among you, I the LORD will make myself known unto him in a vision, and will speak unto him in a dream. My servant Moses is not so, who is faithful in all mine house. With him will I speak mouth to mouth, even apparently, and not in dark speeches; and the similitude of the LORD shall he behold: wherefore then were ye not afraid to speak against my servant Moses? And the anger of the LORD was kindled against them; and he departed. And the cloud departed from off the tabernacle; and, behold, Miriam became leprous, white as snow: and Aaron looked upon Miriam, and, behold, she was leprous.*

> *And Aaron said unto Moses, Alas, my lord, I beseech thee, lay not the sin upon us, wherein we have done foolishly, and wherein we have sinned. Let her not be as one dead, of whom the flesh is half consumed when he cometh out of his mother's womb. And Moses cried unto the LORD, saying, Heal her now, O God, I beseech thee. And the LORD said unto Moses, If her father had but spit in her face, should she not be ashamed seven days? let her be shut out from the camp seven days, and after that let her be received in again. And Miriam was shut out from the camp seven days: and the people journeyed not till Miriam was brought in again." (Num 12:1-15 KJV)*

Moses interceded for those who falsely accused him and prayed for God to have mercy in lieu of judgment. This characteristic is also seen in the life of Stephen the martyr (Acts 7:54-60) and in the life of Christ as depicted on the cross (Luke 23:34).

### III. They are teachable and submissive to God

> *"The meek will he guide in judgment: and the meek will he teach his way." (Psalm 25:9 KJV)*

People who are meek are teachable. They understand it is not possible to "arrive" and do not become content in their knowledge of God. They have a desire to grow and pursue God. Their hearts are flexible and they are willing to submit to the Word of God (Jam 1:21).

### IV. They are content in Christ alone

> *"The meek shall eat and be satisfied." (Psalm 22:26 KJV)*

People who are meek know that satisfaction and delight are temporary apart from Jesus Christ. Their identity and contentment are rooted in what is eternal.

## V. Their confidence in God is unshakable

> *"But the meek shall inherit the earth; and shall delight themselves in the abundance of peace." (Psalm 37:11 KJV)*

Because the meek are rooted and grounded in God, they possess a "quiet spirit" (I Peter 3:4). It is a gentle and peaceful spirit that is confident in the midst of tests or trials.

> *"…their strength is to sit still." (Isaiah 30:7 KJV)*

> *"…in quietness and in confidence shall be your strength."(Isaiah 30:15 KJV)*

## VI. They are lowly in heart

The meek have a deep, inner gratitude towards God and appreciate the gift of life. They understand that life on earth is a gift of trust and use it to live whole-heartedly for God.

> *"Take my yoke upon you, and learn of me; for I am meek and lowly in heart: and ye shall find rest unto your souls."(Matthew 11:29 KJV)*

## VII. They have a stronger private life than public life.

The meek understand that there is power with God in the secret place. They are rooted in God's Word and because it is implanted in their hearts, they have become true practitioners of the Word. These people are more concerned with honoring God than pleasing men.

> *"... and receive with meekness the engrafted word, which is able to save your souls." (James 1:21 KJV)*

The report that Queen Sheba gave of King Solomon should remind believers of the importance of having a stronger private life than public life. When a man's public life is stronger than the strength of his private life, disgrace is inevitable.

> *"And she said to the king, It was a true report that I heard in mine own land of thy acts and of thy wisdom. Howbeit I believed not the words, until I came, and mine eyes had seen it: and, behold, the half was not told me: thy wisdom and prosperity exceedeth the fame which I heard." (I Kings 10:6-7 KJV)*

## BEATITUDE FOUR

> *"Blessed are they which do hunger and thirst after righteousness: for they shall be filled." (Matthew 5:6 KJV)*

> *"Spiritually prosperous are those hungering and thirsting for righteousness, because they themselves shall be filled so as to be completely satisfied." (Matthew 5:6 Went)*

The Greek word for hunger is "peiná," and it means to be famished or starved. The Greek word for thirst is "dipsao," meaning dryness or to be ardently desirous of something. As water and food is to the body, so righteousness is to the spiritual life. Everyone hungers and thirsts for satisfaction in life regardless of race, education level, or economic status. Righteousness is God's way of doing things. When a Christian hungers and thirsts for righteousness they hunger and thirst for His ways.

Think about when you hunger and thirst in your physical body. That hunger or thirst causes you to take action, to actually go and get something to eat or drink. In our spirit, the same thing happens. When we are spiritually hungry, it compels us to go after what satisfies our spirit. God, His Word, and His ways are all one. So when we are spiritually hungry, what satisfies us is God. Righteousness is very satisfying.

> *"As for me, I will behold thy face in righteousness: I shall be satisfied..." (Psalm 17:15 NIV)*

The result of this "hungering" and "thirsting" is the desire to see righteousness in all aspects of life and society. Anything in a person, family, neighborhood, state or nation that lacks the standard of God's righteousness must be confronted in order to change it. In order to see the reign and rule of God in the earth, believers need passion for God burning in their hearts, enabling them to declare war against all injustice, lawlessness, wickedness and all works of darkness.

> *"Of the increase of his government and peace there shall be no end, upon the throne of David, and upon his kingdom, to order it, and to establish it with judgment and with justice from henceforth even for ever. The zeal of the LORD of hosts will perform this."(Isaiah 9:7 KJV)*

Only those who hunger and thirst will be compelled to establish God's kingdom in the earth and to see His righteousness and His ways prevail. There must be a passion to see the living Christ displayed, as He truly is which only comes through an impartation of the Holy Spirit, who is the Spirit of the kingdom. It is with this inner empowerment, that God's justice and judgment will reign supreme. *"Of the increase of his government and peace there shall be no end."* God is committed to seeing His Kingdom increase and every believer is invited to share in its expansion.

> *"Your throne, O God, is forever and ever; A scepter of righteousness is the scepter of Your kingdom. You love righteousness and hate wickedness; Therefore God,*

> *Your God, has anointed You with the oil of gladness more than Your companions." (Psalm 45:6-7 NKJV)*

God's scepter, the authority and right to rule, is a scepter of justice. Justice is impossible without divine anger towards wickedness (John 5:19). Although it is easy to be desensitized in the world today, the truth is that sin offends God and has a tremendous impact on society as a whole. No form of godliness can be exchanged for the power that enables people to experience a transformed life.

*Prayer: God, I ask that my hunger and thirst for spiritual things increase. I want to know you in a deeper way, and to be filled with passion for your name. Help me to discover your assignment for my life and to fulfill my reason for living. I want to see Jesus exalted and his name made famous. I receive strength, power and endurance to fulfill your will for my life. Amen.*

## BEATITUDE FIVE

> "Blessed are the merciful: for they shall obtain mercy." (Matthew 5:7 KJV)

> "Spiritually prosperous are those who are merciful, because they themselves shall be the objects of mercy." (Matthew 5:7 Went)

Mercy never originates with mankind. It begins with God pouring out His mercy – His compassion, love and forgiveness. It is then a person is able to extend this same mercy to others. Those who have trusted in the mercy of God have been saved from death and destruction; God has redeemed them, through Jesus Christ, rather than demanding justice. This is His standard for every Christian.

> "Be ye merciful, as your Father also is merciful."(Luke 6:36 KJV)

When a person gets a revelation of the gravity of what God has done on his or her behalf, the more natural it should be to extend mercy to others. God calls believers blessed for extending mercy, because as it is extended, He guarantees they will also obtain it. Blessed are the merciful, for they shall obtain mercy.

> "And Jesus answering said, A certain man went down from Jerusalem to Jericho, and fell among thieves, which stripped him of his raiment, and wounded him, and departed, leaving him half dead. And by chance there came down a certain priest that way: and when he saw him, he passed by on the other side And likewise a Levite, when he was at the place, came and looked on him, and passed by on the other side. But a certain Samaritan, as he journeyed, came where he was: and when he saw him, he had compassion on him, And went to him, and bound up his wounds, pouring in oil and wine, and set him on his own beast, and brought him to an inn, and took care of him. And on the morrow when he departed, he took out two pence, and gave them to the host, and said unto him, Take care of him; and whatsoever thou spendest more, when I come again, I will repay thee. Which now of these three, thinkest thou, was neighbor unto him that fell among the thieves? And he said, He that showed mercy on him. Then said Jesus unto him, Go, and do thou likewise." (Luke 10:30-37 KJV)

This story is a true reminder of the meaning of the word "mercy." It is a characteristic of God, imparted by His Spirit that enables Christians to extend acts of kindness to others, the deserving and undeserving, while expecting nothing in return. Christianity is best lived through actions that demonstrate the heart of God. The church should be known by mighty deeds of mercy, rather than dogmatic doctrines or external religious formalities. It is "doing good" in its purest form in order to please the Father. Many churches and ministries do good things out of duty or obligation, without a genuine work of mercy in-wrought into the soul by the Holy Spirit. It is only that which is sourced from God that glorifies God. Therefore, mercy has four fundamental characteristics:

- It is the act of kindness given for the sole purpose of revealing the heart of the Father and the nature of Jesus Christ (Matt 5:43-48)
- It is a way of life, obedient to God's Word (Luke 6:27-36)
- It is done out of genuine care for people (Gal 6:10)
- It is a reflection of one's gratitude for God's mercy (Lamentations 3:22-23).

> *"He hath showed thee, O man, what is good; and what doth the LORD require of thee, but to do justly, and to love mercy, and to walk humbly with thy God?" (Micah 6:8 KJV)*

## BEATITUDE SIX

*"Blessed are the pure in heart: for they shall see God." (Matthew 5:8 KJV)*

The first principle that stands out in this beatitude is that Jesus is concerned with the heart. It is not enough to clean up ones act on the outside (Matthew 23:25-26). Jesus Christ did not come to earth to change behavior, but to change the heart of man. The root determines the fruit. If the condition of the heart is right, it will affect everything visible. The purer the heart, the more a Christian can see God as He truly is. Otherwise, the heart is veiled, and Christ cannot be displayed. The heart of fallen man is completely ignorant of God and His ways (Eph 4:18-19). Therefore, to be pure in heart means the condition of ones recreated spirit must be void of all deceit, impurities, mixtures, and biases.

> *"Who shall ascend into the hill of the LORD? Or who shall stand in his holy place? He that hath clean hands,*

*and a pure heart; who hath not lifted up his soul unto vanity, nor sworn deceitfully."(Psalm 24:3-4 KJV)*

King David recognized that a pure heart is one that is free from all falsehood (dishonesty, lies, etc.). It is absolutely truthful and free from deceitfulness. Christianity is a call to all that is true, virtuous, sincere and honest. Even the church must be careful of this heart condition. Anyone who stays in an environment long enough learns the "language" and "behavior" of that environment. People can do and say the right things without their heart being engaged (Matthew. 15:8).

The heart, or the spirit, is where God lives (I Corinthians. 6:19), and all of His dealings with believers take place here. Everything that flows from the Spirit of God is 100% pure. As He works from within ones heart, and it passes through the soul (the mind, emotions and will) of the same person. However, the soulish part of a person, the seat of the personality, has been fashioned by the world's spirit and systems (James 4:4). Just as the optical eye is dependant on the quality or condition of its vision (Luke 11:34-36); so also is the heart in its ability to comprehend truth through the lens of the soul.

Imagine for a moment that you have 20/20 vision, and as a result, you see things as they really are. What happens if you wear sunglasses? Things will not be as clear; they will appear darkened. This is why Christians are to continually renew their minds (Romans 12:2). The heart must be kept free from impurities in order to enlarge its capacity to see God as He really is (2 Corinthians. 4:6). The good news is that as a Christian's heart is purified and focused on Christ, they are able to see Him, and when they see Him, they are able to reflect Him. Otherwise, their efforts will be in vein, because a veiled heart has a distorted view of God (2 Corinthians. 3:18). This work of renewing the mind and purifying the heart never ends, and it is the only way to avoid mixing impurities with all that is received from the Holy Spirit in a person's heart (I Corinthians. 13:12).

> "Beloved, now we are children of God; and it has not yet been revealed what we shall be, but we know that when He is revealed, we shall be like Him, for we shall see Him as He is. And everyone who has this hope in Him purifies himself, just as He is pure."(I John 3:2-3 KJV)

## BEATITUDE SEVEN

> *"Blessed are the peacemakers: for they shall be called the children of God"(Matthew 5:9 KJV)*

Peacemakers are people who bring peace. They naturally long for, work for and sacrifice for peace at all cost. It is fair to say that most people love peace, but there is a difference between loving peace and making peace. Read the following verses:

> "Ye have heard that it hath been said, Thou shalt love thy neighbor, and hate thine enemy. But I say unto you, Love your enemies, bless them that curse you, do good to them that hate you, and pray for them which despitefully use you, and persecute you; That ye may be the children of your Father which is in heaven: for he maketh his sun to rise on the evil and on the good, and sendeth rain on the just and on the unjust." (Matthew 5:43-45 KJV)

In the above verses, Jesus says that peacemakers are called sons of God (children of your Father) and in order to qualify, they must love their enemies, bless those that curse them and pray for those who persecute them. Peacemaking is rooted in destroying enmity between people, which is hostility, bad feelings or tension. God calls Christians to love all people, including those with whom they have challenges, differences, or offenses. There is a blessing that comes when believers choose to be peacemakers. Christians actually have the power to bring peace.

Peacemakers also do everything in their power to restore mankind back to his maker. They understand the ministry of reconciliation and see themselves as ambassadors for Christ. Their experience of the goodness of God compels them to reach out and introduce others to God's grace and kindness (Rom 1:15).

> *"But all things are from God, Who through Jesus Christ reconciled us to Himself [received us into favor, brought us into harmony with Himself] and gave to us the ministry of reconciliation [that by word and deed we might aim to bring others into harmony with Him]. It was God [personally present] in Christ, reconciling and restoring the world to favor with Himself, not counting up and holding against [men] their trespasses [but cancelling them], and committing to us the message of reconciliation (of the restoration to favor). So we are Christ's ambassadors, God making His appeal as it were through us. We [as Christ's personal representatives] beg you for His sake to lay hold of the divine favor [now offered you] and be reconciled to God. For our sake He made Christ [virtually] to be sin Who knew no sin, so that in and through Him we might become [endued with, viewed as being in, and examples of] the righteousness of God [what we ought to be, approved and acceptable and in right relationship with Him, by His goodness]."* (2 Corinthians 5:18-21 AMP)

This virtue of the kingdom produces a different mindset, one that allows a person to see the world through the eyes of eternity. Christians should understand that they are sent by God into this earthly realm with a divine mission to transform the hearts of men (John 17-8). Everything in life is a means to this end. A person's marriage, family, career, wealth, etc. are all tools to be used for the glory of God and His Kingdom. Christians are called to be fully engaged in reaching out to the world in the power and wisdom of the Spirit of God (Galatians 6:13).

> *"And how shall they preach, except they be sent? as it is written, How beautiful are the feet of them that preach the gospel of peace, and bring glad tidings of good things!" (Romans 10:15 KJV)*

The Gospel message was given by God to draw humanity back to Him. God is a peacemaking God; He sacrificed his own Son to reconcile the world to Himself and to one another. If God went to such great lengths to bring peace, then believers should also go to great lengths to bring peace. Peacemakers aim for restoration, harmony, and are continually looking for ways, big or small, to create peace.

> *"If it be possible, as much as lieth in you, live peaceably with all men." (Romans 12:18 KJV)*

## BEATITUDE EIGHT

> *"Blessed are they which are persecuted for righteousness' sake: for theirs is the kingdom of heaven."(Matthew 5:10 KJV)*

> *"You're blessed when your commitment to God provokes persecution. The persecution drives you even deeper into God's kingdom." (Matthew 5:10 MSG)*

The righteousness spoken of in these scriptures is two-fold, and refers to the character of rightness and the work of justice.

## THE CHARACTER OF RIGHTNESS

Scripture reveals that righteousness is the gift of God's own nature and is imparted to a believer in the new-birth (Rom 5:17), thereby placing him in right standing with God. This position is without any work or self-effort. In other words, nothing from a human perspective can enable a person to stand acceptable in

God's presence (Eph 2:8-9). The "gift" of righteousness was given to empower Christians to reign in life (Rom 5:17) and to live righteous lives that are pleasing to God. It is in no way a license to practice sin (Titus 2:11-12). True inward righteousness produces the character of rightness, that is, the desire to live right. Just as the invisible life of the Vine is revealed in the fruit that it produces, so is the life of God revealed through the fruit of a Christian's life.

> *"Little children, let no man deceive you: he that doeth righteousness is righteous, even as he is righteous."(I John 3:7 KJV)*

In a world where so many people live without values and standards, the church must take her rightful place as the light of the world.

> *"In him was life; and the life was the light of men." (John 1:4 KJV)*

When Christianity is practiced without character and a distinct value system, it makes void the power of the gospel in its ability to transform lives. The gospel was designed to produce a difference in people's lives, and to distinguish them from the values and mindsets of the world.

## THE WORKS OF JUSTICE

Works of justice are greatly needed in the body of Christ today. In a world where systemic corruption prevails, the church must rise up and permeate the systems of this world, as the salt of the earth, with justice.

> *"Justice and judgment are the habitation of thy throne: mercy and truth shall go before thy face." (Psalms 89:14 KJV)*

Where lawlessness exists, there is bound to be corruption. When a nation's leaders are corrupt, that nation suffers greatly. Sadly enough, there are countries all around the world where systemic corruption is not only tolerated, but also encouraged as a means of keeping corrupt leaders in power.

> *"When the righteous are in authority, the people rejoice: but when the wicked beareth rule, the people mourn."*
> *(Proverbs 29:2 KJV)*

It is time for Christians to get into positions of power and authority, and to bring with them the values and principles of the Kingdom of God. Every sphere of society needs to be seasoned and preserved with the salt of the earth, meaning Christians.

> *"And the work of righteousness shall be peace; and the effect of righteousness quietness and assurance for ever. And my people shall dwell in a peaceable habitation, and in sure dwellings, and in quiet resting places."*
> *(Isaiah 32:17-18 KJV)*

God's justice in the earth is needed for the sustenance and success of a nation. It brings days of heaven upon the earth and real prosperity that lasts. Those who have committed their lives to establishing justice have found it a rigorous and long journey; nonetheless, their bravery, tenacity and fortitude have inspired millions of others to this end: that one person, with a righteous cause, can change the world and make it a better place.

Justice seeks to eradicate evil by understanding the cause and not just the symptoms. Only the church, as the salt of the earth, has the power to deal with the root cause of systemic corruption. This is how it works. Nations are built on seven pillars. These pillars define the very existence of a nation's identity. Without them, nations cannot possess a "modus-operandi." These pillars are listed as follows: 1) The Political Structure; 2) The Business Structure; 3) The Educational Structure; 4) The Mass Media; 5) The Arts and Entertainment Structure; 6) The Religious Structure; and 7) The Family Structure. Each of these structures is established on value-systems, and all value-systems have their origin in God or Satan. If Satan's values dominate the 7 spheres of any nation, it would mean that the predominant culture of the land is Satanic (1 John 5:19). If this is the case, the belief system of the people will contain values that are opposite and antagonistic to those of the Kingdom of God. Think about it. If mankind is a product of his environment and his belief system is determined by the culture of the day, then whoever controls the value-system controls the nation and its destiny. The gospel of the Jesus Christ must transform not only mankind, but also his environment. This happens by displacing Satan's value-system and replacing it with the value-system of the kingdom of God. This is called the "discipling of nations" (Matthew 28:19).

The kingdom mandate is to disciple all 7 structures with the values of the King and the principles of His Kingdom. The church must intentionally raise righteous people to bring in the values of Christ into all 7 spheres. These structures are the "nets" used to strategically take back the earth and bring in a harvest of souls for God. Those who pursue such a worthy cause show that they care about God's crown-creation and creation itself. They are willing to live beyond self and are willing, if possible, to give their lives for it. They understand that evil prevails, if righteous men do nothing. They see themselves responsible for the salvation of men. These are the men like Nehemiah, Ezra, Joseph and Daniel as well as women like Deborah, Ruth and Esther. These people couldn't standby and watch God's creation disintegrate into despair. They stood up in confidence and as saviors (Obadiah 1:21), and took kingdom responsibility for their nation. Christianity in the 21st century must transcend religious clichés within its four-walls and excel in solving global problems in every field - science, medicine, economics, international relations, politics, education, agriculture, arts and entertainment, etc. Christians have the power and ability to solve every societal ill and injustice. They must translate their faith into tangible solutions and show the world that Jesus is the answer and the only true hope for this world.

## BEATITUDE NINE

> "Blessed are ye, when men shall revile you, and persecute you, and shall say all manner of evil against you falsely, for my sake. Rejoice, and be exceeding glad: for great is your reward in heaven: for so persecuted they the prophets which were before you." (Matthew 5:11-12 KJV)

This type of persecution has to do with the slandering of the tongue. It is an attempt to discredit the name of Christ by discrediting the messenger and his message. It is interesting that those in religious circles are generally the ones who speak evil about other Christians. Even in the days of Jesus, the religious were the number one contender with His ministry. In this day and age, religious people are the chief obstacle, chief enemy and chief destroyer of every true work of the spirit. Satan, the arch-accuser and arch blasphemer, finds easy access into religious institutions and uses this access to discredit the name of Christ. Both the media and entertainment industries are perfect ground for accomplishing this aim.

Religion is Satan's workshop in hindering the work of Christ. It takes an in-wrought work of the Holy Spirit to produce a meek and quiet spirit (I Peter 3:4), and Christians must respond to all accusations with the Lamb Spirit of the Lord Jesus.

> "He was oppressed, and he was afflicted, yet he opened not his mouth: he is brought as a lamb to the slaughter, and as a sheep before her shearers is dumb, so he openeth not his mouth." (Isaiah 53:7 KJV)

Jesus knew that His Father's vindication of Him was better than any human government. He made no haste to lay claims of His rightness, but left all judgment to God. It is also important for believers, when falsely accused, to have faith in the God of justice. Remember how the nation of Israel accused Jesus falsely and how He was ridiculed and humiliated before the world; yet was controlled from within by the government of the Holy Spirit. This was a true manifestation of His lamb-nature proving He had absolute confidence in the One who vindicates all. Only those who are truly broken before God can respond to false accusations in the manner that Jesus did.

> "And they that passed by reviled him, wagging their heads, And saying, Thou that destroyest the temple, and buildest it in three days, save thyself. If thou be the Son of God, come down from the cross. Likewise also the chief priests mocking him, with the scribes and elders..." (Matthew 27:39-41 KJV)

Always keep in mind the reason for true persecution. As believers hunger and thirst for righteousness, they are filled. As they are filled, their hunger for God begins to be satisfied and it overflows with mercy, a pure heart, and with the power to make peace. The result is persecution for this very righteousness. This is the same persecution that Jesus experienced. It is not persecution that is self-induced from bad choices, being irresponsible or being ignorant, but as a result of reflecting the very nature of Jesus Christ. It is for His sake, and it will refine a person as gold, if they endure and faint not.

## THE BEATITUDES AND OUR SALTINESS

Often people tend to separate the beatitudes (Matt 5:3-12), from Jesus referring to Christians as the salt of the earth (Matt 5:13), but they must go hand in hand to fully understand the message. Jesus was communicating that the beatitudes are the salt with which believers season the world. It makes sense that if Christians lose their saltiness, being poor in spirit, merciful, and pure in heart etc; they lose their relevance as the salt of the earth. These are the qualities that make people as beautiful as Christ, and distinguish them from the world. They reveal who Jesus Christ really is and show how to exchange worldly values for the values that can only be obtained in Christ. It is the character of Christ that mirrors to the world its deficits and ultimately draws them into the saving knowledge of Jesus Christ.

It is amazing how much emphasis is being placed on other things, when the emphasis of every church should be how to put on Christ in practice (Gal 3:27). People need to ask themselves, "Am I more like Christ in all aspects of life?" "Am I as merciful, as meek, as pure, as thirsty after justice; do I mourn as He mourned?" The church is losing the world for Christ because it lacks the power that manifests in authentic Christianity. The early church never called themselves Christians; the world called them Christians because they behaved like Christ. They were new men created after God in righteousness and true holiness. To win the world, people must have the fruits of a changed life. The beatitudes are known as the values of the kingdom of God, and as the salt of the earth, believers should bring this saltiness into every sphere of society.

## HINDRANCE THREE
## "SABOTAGE"

Self-sabotage character traits are the third hindrance to a salted life, and refer to those who betray Christ by their lifestyle. This is a major hindrance that weakens ones effectiveness as the salt of the earth, and makes the gospel powerless due to the lack of a Christ-like lifestyle. The biggest question everyone is thinking is, "Is anyone really living the life?" It is dangerous that Christian living is not taken seriously anymore. Too many people hide behind a set of Christian beliefs in their mind without the corresponding actions that should follow such beliefs. So much emphasis has been placed on the fallen state of man, being "sinners saved by grace," which deny the very power God gave us to disconnect from the power of sin (which is rooted in self). Self is the greatest enemy to Christian living, the work of the Spirit in a person's heart, and to the body of Christ as a whole.

> "And if thy hand offend thee, cut it off: it is better for thee to enter into life maimed, than having two

*hands to go into hell, into the fire that never shall be quenched: Where their worm dieth not, and the fire is not quenched. And if thy foot offend thee, cut it off: it is better for thee to enter halt into life, than having two feet to be cast into hell, into the fire that never shall be quenched: Where their worm dieth not, and the fire is not quenched. And if thine eye offend thee, pluck it out: it is better for thee to enter into the kingdom of God with one eye, than having two eyes to be cast into hell fire: Where their worm dieth not, and the fire is not quenched. For every one shall be salted with fire, and every sacrifice shall be salted with salt Salt is good: but if the salt have lost his saltiness, wherewith will ye season it? Have salt in yourselves, and have peace one with another." (Mark 9:43-50 KJV)*

These "sins" should never be downplayed as weaknesses or habits (Heb 12:1). There needs to be a true conviction of the Holy Spirit in regards to sin and how it is viewed from God's perspective (Gen 39:9). True freedom from the power of sin lies within reach of those who sincerely desire it (Rom 6). Sinful habits in ones life become a self-inflicted entrapment (James 1:14-15), and a perfect breeding ground for demonic activity (1Jn 5:18). These habits condition the soul, and, beginning with the mind, the flesh is formed. This is called the fleshly mind (Col 2:18), or the carnal mind (Rom 8:6-7). It is then that the body, as a slave of the soul, becomes the vehicle for the "works of the flesh", (Galatians 5:19-21, 24) which are sourced in the mind (Romans 7:5).

Nothing defiles the beauty of Christ like sin. Nothing destroys the inner workings of the Holy Spirit like sin. Nothing breeds confusion and darkness as sin and nothing destroys ones power to witness, as well as mocks God, like sin (II Sam 12:13-14). Sin drains spiritual vitality and brings death to ones spiritual life.

So what's up with sin? Are people internally wired to sin (Romans 6:2)? Are there things in humanity of their own making or the making of others that causes them to stumble? Let's look at it from a personal level. Did you know that although your human spirit is recreated in Christ (2 Corinthians 5:17), that your soul (mind, emotions, will) and your body are still under the influence of the old Adamic life? (Romans 6:6, Ephesians 4:22, Romans 6:12-13, Romans 7:5) Did you know that the cross is not just the place for salvation through the blood of Christ (Romans 5:9), but also where the influence of sin in the soul and the body are to be dealt with? This is foreshadowed in the Old Testament in Numbers 21:6-9. The venom of the serpent permeated the whole being (I Thessalonians. 5:23), and the work of the cross is the remedy for it. In the soul is self-consciousness and in the body is sense-consciousness. These were formed from the influence of the world (James 4:4). The cross and its power (I Corinthians. 1:18) must be applied to all that "causes us to stumble." Anything that offends ones fellowship with God, and with the stability, durability and immutability of that fellowship (Genesis 5:22 Amp), must be severed (Hebrews 4:12). As Christians stand in faith in the finished work of the cross, the Holy Spirit will make true the reality of the cross in its power to set free from sin.

## CAUSING ONE TO STUMBLE

The life believers live as representatives of the Kingdom is the Life of the Kingdom. What they model before the world and fellow Christians is very important to the heart of God. The passage Mark 9:42-50 must be fully opened up by the Holy Spirit so as to see the seriousness of the message and heed the warnings within its pages.

> *"And whosoever shall offend one of these little ones that believe in me, it is better for him that a milestone were hanged about his neck, and he were cast into the sea." (Mark 9:42 KJV)*

The lifestyle of a Christian will either cause the world to believe in Christ and the "little ones" to stand strong for Him or cause them to stumble. The body of Christ is the only visible Jesus in the earth. The power to convince the world of a living Savior is directly relational to the lifestyle that is modeled before them.

> *"In Him was Life; and the Life was the Light of men."*
> *(John 1:4 KJV)*

Just as the invisible Life of the Vine (John. 15:1-2) must translate into tangible fruit; so must the Life of God in the believer translate into a visible lifestyle if they are to be relevant. If believers profess a gospel with power to transform lives (Rom. 1:16), yet live contrary to the fruit of a changed life; they make the gospel void and its power a lie.

> *"For although they hold a form of piety {true religion}, they deny and reject and are strangers to the power of it {their conduct belies the genuineness of their profession}. Avoid all such people {turn away from them}." (2 Timothy. 3:5 AMP)*

As citizens of the Kingdom of God, the way believers live out their daily lives is very important. They represent the very kingdom that is ruled and governed by Jesus Christ. It is their lifestyle that sustains the influence of the church in the earth today.

> *"Your very lives are a letter that anyone can read by just looking at you. Christ Himself wrote it- not with ink but with God's living Spirit; not chiseled into stone, but carved into human lives- and we publish it." (2 Corinthians. 3:2-3 The Message)*

Sinful habits and attitudes don't only affect those who have them; it affects everything and everyone else around them (2 Samuel 12:14 KJV). All behavior, directly or indirectly, sheds light or veils the light of God. It can empower the work of the kingdom or hinder it. Jesus said in Mark 9:42, that if severe consequences accompany lifestyles that cause new believers to stumble; how much greater the consequences accompany those who hinder the unsaved from coming to Christ? The church must no longer give excuses and take full responsibility for her lack of power in revealing the visibility of the life of Christ to a lost world. The power of the cross is to flow and free people from works of darkness, yet it's dependent upon how believers live for Christ. They must not side with Satan in blinding the minds of the unsaved and devaluing the standards of God by making light of sin (2 Tim. 2:19).

*"And if thy hand offends thee, cut it off."* The word hand represents works, which translates into those who seek earthly things and live for the things of this world. Life is so much more than making a living (Matt. 6:25). Yes, God requires people to work and take care of their families, but it is still not the main purpose for living. People are called to live beyond self. Think about how many people get an education to enhance self, get a job to preserve self, get married for self, and have children for self. This is a failed life in the eyes of God. Every one of the things mentioned above can be pursued with Christ at the center. Christ needs to be the reason behind everything believer's do in life. In both the old and new testaments of scripture, man's ability to accomplish great things for God was a direct result of His presence upon or within them. Man also must recognize His dependence upon God as revealed in Moses (Ex. 33:13-16), in Christ (Jn. 5:19; Luke 6:12), in the early Church (Acts 6:4) and in Paul the Apostle (1 Cor. 15:10; Col. 1:29; Eph 3:16).

Do people realize that things, which appeal to the senses, can only penetrate only as far as the soul? Whether it is a certain type of music, lights, stage props, etc., all of these things can bring men to the Holy Place but never into the Holy of Holies. Only the Holy Spirit's work in a person's heart can produce a work of the Spirit in him. These sensory things have their place, yet nothing on the outside can produce His work, for He, the Holy Spirit, works from within.

"Hand" deals with all labor related to the acquisition of natural things at the expense of spiritual things. It has to do with the over-occupation with the cares of this life at the expense of the kingdom.

It is the seeking to preserve one's life at all cost. *"And Satan answered the Lord and said, yea, all that a man hath will he give for his life" (Job 2:4 KJV)*. Anything sourced in Christ is acquired under His governance; established on His values, carried out for His glory and used for the influence of His kingdom.

*"And if thy foot offend thee, cut if off."* The foot speaks of the pride of life (I Jn. 2:15-16). It refers to those who acquired fame, prestige, wealth, power and position and use it to look great in the eyes of men rather than influencing the world with kingdom values. These are people who applaud themselves on their own achievements and use them to enhance their own self-worth. People can be externally great yet internally bankrupt at the same time.

> *"And thou say in thine heart, my power and the might of mine hand hath gotten me this wealth." (Deuteronomy 8:17 KJV)*

God desires these things to be used for HIS glory. He wants the center of every ambition and achievement to be used as a platform to make Him known to a lost world. And even behind all success, God wants nothing to hinder ones personal walk with Him, whether it be lawful or unlawful.

> *"I can do anything I want to if Christ has not said no, but some of these things aren't good for me. Even if I am allowed to do them, I'll refuse to if I think they might get such a grip on me that I can't easily stop when I want to. For instance, take the matter of eating. God has given us an appetite for food and stomachs to digest it. But that doesn't mean we should eat more than we need. Don't think of eating as important because someday God will do away with both stomachs and food." (1 Corinthians 6:12-13 TLB)*

So even something as significant as "food" can become a hindrance to ones spiritual life? It is true. No church can be truly spiritual in dealing with self and the forces of darkness without prayer and fasting. Any church without a praying and fasting culture has too many alternatives and substitutes for spiritual things (Isa. 56:9). God is too great to become "something on the side" that is added to the other things in a person's life. He must be the center and focus in which everything else revolves.

> "Enoch walked in habitual fellowship with God… 300 years." (Genesis 5:22 AMP)

God wants His children to live in unbroken fellowship with Him, but the pride of this life and the deceitfulness of riches will choke the love for God out of ones heart. It is never too late to return back to our "first-love" and do the "first-works."

*"And if thy eye offends thee, pluck it out."* If the vision of the eye is distorted, it affects how one sees in life (Luke 11:33-36). The eye represents the "lusts of the eyes."

> "Then the devil took Him up to a high mountain and showed Him all the kingdoms of the habitable world in a moment of time {in the twinkling of an eye}. And he said to Him, to you I will give all this power and authority and their glory (all their magnificence, excellence, preeminence; dignity, and grace), for it has been turned over to me, and I give it to whomever I will." (Luke 4:5-6 AMP)

Jesus' eyes saw only what was in the Father's heart *(Jn. 4:34)*. His single mindedness is an example to all Christians, as well as His hunger to please the Father, which exceeded the hunger of His physical body (Luke 4:3-4). His desire for the glory of the Father exceeded His quest for the glory of this world. All sin and shame, all shortcomings were laid on Jesus Christ and it is every Christian's faith in the finished work that counts. The outworking of the finished work starts when one understands His love for him or her and out of the revelation of that love long to please Him in all things (1Jn. 4:19).

Without His love at the center of their worship and faith, believers simply become religious. A person's heartfelt love for God will not allow them to take Him or His word for granted, but will draw them closer to Him and His ways.

## CUT IT OFF; PLUCK IT OUT

The lust in the soul, which is the "love to sin", manifesting as the works of the flesh in the body, must be dealt with from the root. As Christians appropriate Romans 6:2 by faith, as a finished work, faithfully live out Romans 6:12 in daily life, and simultaneously learn to walk in the Spirit (Gal. 5:25), strengthening the spirit-man by use (Eph 3:16) and obeying the laws of the spirit-life (Rom 8:2), they will come to know true freedom in Christ Jesus. In the light of the truth of such freedom, no one remains yoked or bound, or in view of God's mercies chooses to remain ignorant and helpless. Rather, every Christian should take full advantage of their redemptive rights in Christ Jesus and walk on to complete victory.

## SALTED WITH FIRE

> "For every one shall be salted with fire." (Mark 9:49 KJV)

The entire body of Christ must realize the enormous responsibility of winning this world to Jesus Christ and that the urgency of the times demands a radical work of the cross. This work of the cross should produce a real transformation that results in the visible character of Christ and the values of His kingdom. This fire must judge and purge today's church from idolatry and eventually thrust her out to win the world for Christ.

> "For the time is come that judgment must begin at the house of God: and if it first begin at us, what shall the end be of them that obey not the gospel of God? And if

> the righteous scarcely be saved, where shall the ungodly and the sinner appear?" (1 Peter 4:17-18 KJV)

God will use fire as a seasoning to cleanse His house, and the church will come forth as gold (Mal 3:3-4). God loves people too much to leave them the way they are, but people must choose to side with God and consent to the work of the cross being carried out in their lives.

> "In that day shall the branch of the LORD be beautiful and glorious, and the fruit of the earth shall be excellent and comely for them that are escaped of Israel. And it shall come to pass, that he that is left in Zion, and he that remaineth in Jerusalem, shall be called holy, even every one that is written among the living in Jerusalem: When the Lord shall have washed away the filth of the daughters of Zion, and shall have purged the blood of Jerusalem from the midst thereof by the spirit of judgment, and by the spirit of burning." (Isaiah 4:2-4 KJV)

To win the world, Christ must be put on in practice (Gal. 3:27). His beauty must become the beauty of the Church and His passion must be hers as well. Heaven's fire must purge her from everything and anything that doesn't look like Christ and thrust her out into the world to do the father's will. It is time for the fear of God to reign in the hearts of men.

> "…Let us cleanse ourselves from all filthiness of the flesh and Spirit, perfecting holiness in the fear of God." (2 Corinthians 7:1 KJV)

## EVERY SACRIFICE SHALL BE SALTED WITH SALT

> "… and every sacrifice shall be salted with salt." (Mark 9:49 KJV)

The cross was God's perfect path for Christ, and without which, Christianity would have never existed. If there were no cross, there would be no Christianity. God saves and delivers and makes people whole, but all that work serves as a means to an end, and it was given to serve humanity. Christ poured out His soul unto death for the human race, and we should, in turn, lay down our lives for the sake of a lost world.

> *"For the love of Christ constraineth us; because we thus judge, that if one died for all,...that they which live should not henceforth live unto themselves, but unto him which died for them and rose again." (2 Corinthians 5:14-15 KJV)*

Compelled by His love, no sacrifice seems too much to give. The church should know that discipleship necessitates a cross-carried in the weight of God's love for us. May the mighty Holy Spirit reveal the Father's love as demonstrated in Christ Jesus, that believer's may be filled with this fullness. Humanity should never shrink back to save her own life (Job 2:4), but place everything on the cross (Mark 15:30). There is salt in laying down ones life to please Him. Those who sacrifice for Christ and the cause of His kingdom are truly living, and as they drink of His love, they will be compelled to live for Him in a way that will shake the very powers of darkness.

> *"Peter took him in hand, protesting, 'Impossible, Master! That can never be!'" But Jesus didn't swerve. "Peter, get out of my way. Satan, get lost. You have no idea how God works" (Matthew 16: 22-23 MSG)*

Peter lived for self-preservation and almost became a snare to Christ. A gospel of ease and self-preservation will always hinder the church from fulfilling her purpose. She must be willing to suffer with Christ, not wanting to profit from Him (like Judas Iscariot). It is time for the church to rise up and become a house of prayer, to live in holiness and purity, and to walk in the power and authority given to her through Jesus Christ.

## CHRISTLIKENESS; OUR SALTINESS

*"Salt is good; but if the salt have lost his saltiness, wherewith will ye season it? Have salt in yourselves..."*
*(Mark 9:50 KJV)*

Christ-likeness is the believer's business. The strategic blueprint of every local church is to mature believers into Christ-likeness as the means of restoring the earth back to God (Eph. 4:11-13). Too much emphasis has been placed on the frailty of human nature, the fallen state of man, and it has left loopholes for excuses and delayed authentic discipleship. Pastors will be held accountable for whether or not they have empowered the body of Christ to press on to the mark of the prize of the high calling in Christ Jesus. Shouldn't leaders raise the standards of God rather than lowering His standards to suit today's lifestyle? Isn't the power of God available to make the church true representatives of Christ? The answer is yes.

The spiritual hunger to become like Christ should exceed all other desires of life if significant impact for Him is going to be accomplished. Until the church is distinct from the world, the world won't be different from the church. A "mixed multitude" is the cause for a lack of standards today. It has created an attitude of "anything goes" and led to all behavior being acceptable in the name of "false love" and "false unity." Even in the midst of such weak standards, it does not negate the fact that there are non-negotiable truths, absolutes, and foundations upon which the church was established.

What happens when Christians lose their relevance? They get trampled underfoot of men and become of no value. This must not be allowed to happen. Christians must put on the beatitudes of Christ and become the light of the world, a city set on a hill for all to see. There is no more time for excuses. It is time to take full responsibility for personal transformation by confirming to the image of God as the means to displacing satanic value-systems and restoring those of the kingdom. This must become the priority of every believer, every local church, and the body of Christ throughout the world.

# Chapter 5
# SEASONING THE WORLD WITH LOVE
## "THE NATURE OF THE KING AND HIS KINGDOM"

> *"For God so loved the world that he gave his only begotten son, that whosoever believeth in him should not perish but have everlasting life." (John 3:16 KJV)*

If the world could see the love of Christ in all of its fullness, their hearts would melt and they would be won over by such love. The key, however, lies with His representatives. Only those who have experienced His great love can give it to others, because it is the Holy Spirit who floods a Christian's heart with love (Romans 5:5). To make Christ known, one must personally know Him, and this only happens by revelation of the Holy Spirit (Gal 1:15-16). A lot of Christians know about the historical Christ, through going to church and reading books about Him, but Christ was not meant to be studied; He was meant to be known, in a personal, intimate way that reaches the core of a person's heart. It is not enough to mentally agree with the facts of who He is; there must be experiential knowledge that is gained through the Spirit of God.

> *"Wherefore of these men which have companied with us all the time that the Lord Jesus went in and out among us, beginning from the baptism of John, unto that same day that he was taken up from us; must one be ordained to be a witness with us of his resurrection." (Acts 1: 21-22 KJV)*

In these scriptures, Peter, by the Holy Spirit, was given a specific qualification for Apostleship. He had to be a "witness of His resurrection" (Acts 1:21). In other words, he had to have personal, first-hand experience of the life and ministry of Christ in order to function in the office of an Apostle. *"And ye also shall bear witness, because ye have been with me from the beginning" (John 15:27).* In the time of the early apostles, the only people who were able to speak for Christ were the eyewitnesses of His works, especially His death, burial and resurrection (I Corinthians 15:3).

## THE ESSENCE OF PENTECOST

> *"But ye shall receive power, after that the Holy Ghost is come upon you: and ye shall be witnesses unto me both in Jerusalem, and in all Judaea, and in Samaria, and unto the uttermost part of the earth." (Acts 1:8 KJV)*

The main reason for receiving the Holy Spirit is to make individuals witnesses OF Christ, so they can become witnesses FOR Christ. The Holy Spirit is the witness bearer (John 15:26), and was sent as the Father's gift to the church. He was not given for experiences or self-centered reasons, but to reveal Christ as He truly is. The Holy Spirit is able to place believers in the same position as the disciples, journeying with Christ throughout his life and ministry. He gives the same encounters that the disciples had with Jesus, through the Word of God, in order to make present day believers eye witnesses as the disciples of old.

> *"This Jesus hath God raised up; whereof we all are witnesses." (Acts 2:32)*

> *"And killed the Prince of life, who God hath raised from the dead; whereof we are witnesses." (Acts 3:15)*

> *"For we cannot but speak the things which we have seen and heard." (Acts 4:20 KJV)*

> *"And with great power gave the apostles witness of the resurrection of the Lord Jesus ..." (Acts 4:33 KJV)*

> *"And we are his witnesses of these things; and so is also the Holy Ghost, whom God hath given to them that obey him." (Acts 5:32 KJV)*

Reading the above scriptures you may say, "How can I be an eye witness if I wasn't born during that time?" Well, think about this. King David wasn't alive during the life of Jesus here on earth. Even so, King David saw Jesus, His life, His sufferings, His cross, His death, His descent into hell and His resurrection (Ps 16:8-10; Acts 2:25-31; Ps 110:1; Acts 2:34-35; Ps 22:1, 7-8, 16, 18; Ps 24: 7-10; Ps 69:21; Ps 88: 6-8). Think about all the other prophets that lived before the cross who saw the Christ (John 8:56). In fact, every book that was written in the Old Testament points toward the life and death of Jesus Christ (Luke 24:25-27).

> *"Of which salvation the prophets have enquired and searched diligently, who prophesied of the grace that should come unto you: Searching what, or what manner of time the Spirit of Christ which was in them did signify, when it testified beforehand the sufferings of Christ, and the glory that should follow." (1 Peter 1:10-11 KJV)*

Just as the Holy Spirit made Jesus Christ real to the prophets who lived thousands of years before His death, He also makes the death, burial and resurrection of Christ real to Christians today. The Holy Spirit, as the Spirit of revelation and understanding, uses the Word of God to illuminate truth in their recreated spirits (1 Co 2:10-12; Pr 20:27) and opens the eyes of their hearts (Eph 1:18). This is what allows believers to hold these truths with such conviction (1 Thess. 1:5). These truths cause a literal transformation to take place, resulting in believers becoming living witnesses of Him. The Spirit of God can take people back in time and reveal to them the finished work of Christ. Only then can Christians witness for Christ in power and undeniable proof (Acts 1:3). Although spiritual power and tongues and mighty works are possible only through the Holy

Spirit, the true purpose of Acts 1:8 is to make Christians witnesses OF Christ so as to make them witnesses FOR Christ.

## GOD IS LOVE

It is true that those who are in Christ Jesus are born of God, and those born of God are born of His love, for God is love. The love of God has been lavishly poured into our hearts by the Holy Spirit - (Rom 5:5). It is also true that one must possess a revelation of the height and depth, the length and breadth of the love of God that transcends mere knowledge (Eph 3:18-19). The personal understanding of the fullness of God's love must compel believers to live by the same standard. *"For the love of Christ constrained us; because we thus judge, that if one died for all, then were all dead. And that he died for all, that they which live should not henceforth live unto themselves, but unto him which died for them, and rose again" (II Corinthians 5:14-15 KJV).* It is the very love of God that should move believers to walk in this love. Just as Christ so loved the world that He gave up His life, not living for Himself, Christians must give up their own lives, for the sake of others, rather than living for self.

## THE SACRIFICIAL LOVE OF CHRIST

> *"Greater love hath no man than this that a man lay down his life for his friends." (John 15:13 KJV)*

The love of Christ was demonstrated through a great sacrifice. If the world could see, firsthand, all that pertained to the sufferings of Christ and how He poured out His soul unto death, and how it was connected to them, they would bow down and yield to His lordship with ease. Such love is inconceivable when grasped by the human mind, primarily because it is so different from the love humanity is able to offer. It takes God Himself, through His Spirit, to reveal how deeply He loved the world, and became man (Heb 2:14); died a death by taking upon Himself the venom of the serpent (Num 21:6-9; John 3:14), and altering His nature as God laid upon

Him the iniquity of all. The sin of the entire world was laid on His Spirit and He was found guilty, sent to Hades, and there he bore the full weight of God's wrath against sin. All of this, He did in the behalf of mankind. How could a person, in full view of such love, remain unchanged? How could those, who profess His name, live unto themselves rather than for Him?

> "But God commendeth his love toward us, in that, while we were yet sinners, Christ died for us. For if, when we were enemies, we were reconciled to God by the death of his Son..." (Rom 5:8,10 KJV)

This perfect love of God; must be experienced in order to be carried and given out by a Christian. Every true revelation of the Spirit leads to impartation, which leads to transformation, which leads to manifestation. Believers must embody the love of Christ in all aspects of life.

## LOVING ONE ANOTHER

> "This is my commandment, that ye love one another, as I have loved you." (John 15:12 KJV)

> "A new commandment I give unto you, that ye love one another; as I have loved you, that ye also love one another. By this shall all men know that ye are my disciples, if ye have love one to another." (John 13:34-35 KJV)

> "Hereby perceive we the love of God, because he laid down his life for us: and we ought to lay down our lives for the brethren." (I John 3:16 KJV)

> "Beloved, if God so loved us, we ought also to love one another. No man hath seen God at any time. If we love one another, God dwelleth in us, and his love is perfected in us." (I John 4:11-12 KJV)

The love of Christ must first be displayed among the body of Christ in the earth. The reason this difficulty exists is because of issues in the soul. To love as Christ loved, people must see as He sees. There is not one human soul who is 100% free of impurities, duplicities and some measure of bias. Jesus said, however, that His judgment is just because he seeks the father's will and not His (John 5:30 KJV). Until people are seen through the eyes of Christ, they cannot love as He loved. It is only through Christ that one can learn to lay down their lives for one another.

> *Yea, and if I be offered upon the sacrifice and service of your faith, I joy, and rejoice with you all. For I have no man likeminded, who will naturally care for your state. For all seek their own, not the things which are Jesus Christ's." (Phil 2:17, 20-21 KJV)*

Laying down ones life for Christ is laying down ones life for those He died for. It is service to others that proves ones service to God. This is the standard of authentic Christianity and was practiced by the early church.

> *"Because for the work of Christ he was nigh unto death, not regarding his life, to supply your lack of service toward me." (Philippians 2:30 KJV)*

It is important to ask oneself, "What proof validates my love for Christ? How do I manifest that love in today's world?"

## THE CHARACTER OF LOVE

> *"Love suffers long and is kind; love does not envy; love does not parade itself, is not puffed up; does not behave rudely, does not seek its own, is not provoked, thinks no evil; does not rejoice in iniquity, but rejoices in the truth…" (1 Corinthians 13:4-6 NKJV)*

God's kind of love is not a feeling; it is a behavior that is acquired through practice. It is through practice that habits are formed and attitudes are sharpened. In the new-birth, God's love was imparted into believer's hearts in seed form (Rom 5:5), but this virtue must be cultivated and grow as it is worked out in practice. *"And walk in love, as Christ also hath loved us, and hath given himself for us an offering and a sacrifice to God for a sweet smelling savor" (Eph 5:2 KJV)*. Habits are not randomly formed; they are formed by repeatedly doing the same thing, and growing in God's love is no exception. It is only through a lifestyle of practice that will build and solidify this kingdom virtue in the believer's life. It is practice, even when not comfortable or favorable that leads to character formation. Christians must clothe themselves with the love of God in order to mirror it to the world.

> *"And over all these virtues put on love, which binds them all together in perfect unity." (Colossians 3:14 NIV)*

> *"And regardless of what else you put on, wear love. It's your basic, all-purpose garment. Never be without it." (Colossians 3:14 MSG)*

## LOVE SUFFERS LONG

The Greek word "Makrothumia" is best described by the following list of words: patience, endurance, constancy, forbearance, perseverance and diligence. It has to do with a steadfast attitude of faith in spite of overwhelming and trying circumstances.

> *"To them who by patient continuance in well doing seek for glory and honor and immortality, eternal life." (Romans 2:7 KJV)*

This word encompasses a disciplined life of faith, unshaken in the midst of unfavorable or challenging situations. It can be compared to people who stick with God's Word and fully obey it without wavering. These are people who would rather suffer the reproaches of Christ than enjoy the riches of Egypt for a moment (Heb 11:25-26). These do not take the path of least resistance. No matter the weight of pain or the cost involved in following Christ, they remain steadfast. It describes those who endure suffering as victors and not victims, whose internal fortitude outweighs their outward circumstances and whose joy overshadows their pain (Heb 12:3). Have you met people like this? They keep at the Word, unleashing their faith with boldness. They say what God says and see what God sees. It may even be difficult to see they are passing through difficult times, because their faith overcomes the world.

> *"And now I want each of you to extend that same intensity toward a full-bodied hope, and keep at it till the finish. Don't drag your feet. Be like those who stay the course with committed faith and then get everything promised to them." (Hebrews 6:11-12 MSG)*
>
> *"And so, after he had patiently endured, he obtained the promise." (Hebrews 6:15 KJV)*

This is a great virtue in the Kingdom of God. Christians are called to suffer long and to stand firm in the fight of faith. It is easy to neglect steadfastness in the midst of a fast-paced culture where everyone wants things now, but nevertheless, this is part of walking in love. This attitude will distinguish believers from the world and bring glory to Christ, as a living and merciful Savior who greatly rewards those who put their trust in Him.

The word "Makrothumia" also means possessing an attitude of forbearance toward ill treatment from others, including those closest to a person. *"Put on therefore, as the elect of God, holy and beloved, bowels of mercies, kindness, humbleness of mind, meekness, longsuffering; forbearing one another, and forgiving one another, if any man have a quarrel against any: even as Christ forgave you, so also do ye" (Col 3:12 -13 KJV).* This also must be cultivated through practice. Offenses will always be present but Christians are called, and able, to walk in love and extend the mercy of Christ, even as He extended mercy towards His church.

> *"With all lowliness and meekness, with longsuffering, forbearing one another in love." (Ephesians 4:2)*

## LOVE IS KIND

> *"Put on therefore ... kindness." (Colossians 3:11 KJV)*

This virtue of the Kingdom deals with acts of kindness, providing something beneficial to someone in need. It involves helping, assisting or aiding someone with a particular necessity; being hospitable, generous and considerate of others, as well as alleviating pain and suffering, are inclusive in this word kindness (Eph 4:32). *"... for he is kind unto the unthankful and the evil." (Luke 6:35 KJV)* Christians are called to extend acts of kindness to both the believers and unbelievers. This is the attitude that mirrors God's love to the world. It is going beyond sharing the good news, but demonstrating it in a tangible and real way.

## THE LAW OF KINDNESS

> *"When the ear heard me, then it blessed me; and when the eye saw me, it gave witness to me: Because I delivered the poor that cried, and the fatherless, and him that had none to help him. The blessing of him that was ready to perish came upon me: and I caused the widow's heart to sing for joy. I put on righteousness, and it clothed me: my judgment was as a robe and a diadem. I was eyes to the blind, and feet were I to the lame. I was a father to the poor: and the cause which I knew not I searched out. And I brake the jaws of the wicked, and plucked the spoil out of his teeth. Then I said, I shall die in my nest, and I shall multiply my days as the sand. My root was spread out by the waters, and*

> *the dew lay all night upon my branch. My glory was fresh in me, and my bow was renewed in my hand. Unto me men gave ear, and waited, and kept silence at my counsel. After my words they spake not again; and my speech dropped upon them. And they waited for me as for the rain; and they opened their mouth wide as for the latter rain. If I laughed on them, they believed it not; and the light of my countenance they cast not down."*
> (Job 29:11-25 KJV)

As the salt of the earth, believers have the responsibility of fulfilling the Abrahamic covenant in practice. Those who look forward to serving humanity with justice and righteousness will be empowered with the resources needed to achieve such aims. It is time to bless the world with the kindness and goodness of Christ; it is time to meet their needs and show them a Savior who cares. All Christians should see themselves as a channel of God's love, flowing unto mankind through acts of mercy and grace (Titus 3:4,6). Life is beautiful and worth living when it is lived to serve humanity with the character of the king and the values of His kingdom.

## LOVE IS NOT ENVIOUS

Envy can be defined as a state of ill will toward someone, because of real or presumed advantage that is experienced by such a person (Louw and Nida Greek English Lexicon of the New Testament). Envy produces a strong feeling of resentment due to the accolades, acquisitions or achievements of someone else. Often, people are envious because they think others don't deserve what they have and think they themselves deserve it more. Thayer's Greek Lexicon defines it as to be "absolutely heated or to boil with jealousy." This is very far from the nature of God. God's love sincerely desires the best for everyone. It rejoices at the success, promotion and progress of others. It even desires that others become greater than themselves. *"Be kindly affectioned one to another with brotherly love; in honor preferring one another" (Rom 12:10 KJV).* Christians are to celebrate and be pleased with the success of others and never give room to the enemy to sow seeds of bitterness (James 3:14; Gal 5:26).

> *"Let nothing be done through strife or vainglory; but in lowliness of mind let each esteem other better than themselves. Look not every man on his own things, but every man also on the things of others." (Philippians 2:3-4 KJV)*

If a person is truly living for the kingdom, and all that they are doing is for Christ and not themselves, there would be no room for rivalry or jealousy. It is important to avoid worldly competition and comparisons, which are both childish and carnal (1 Cor. 3:3). Envy is devilish in nature, because it causes strife, divisions and contentions. When people rejoice and celebrate the progress of others, it makes room for them to progress as well.

## LOVE IS NOT BOASTFUL

Love is not boastful or vainglorious; it doesn't brag or parade itself haughtily. There is nothing pushy or forceful about the love of God. It is not full of ambition or high-minded.

> *"Be of the same mind one toward another. Mind not high things, but condescend to men of low estate. Be not wise in your own conceits." (Romans 12: 16 KJV)*

Being boastful is rooted in pride, because it reveals itself in an attitude of superiority. It is one seeing themselves as better as or more important than others around them. The Bible warns against this by informing believers not to "think of themselves more highly than they ought." Even within the church, it is easy to see pastors or church leaders carry themselves in a way that reveals this attitude. Authentic, Christ-like humility has nothing to do with this mindset or attitude (Phil 2:5-9). Jesus was the greatest of all, yet a servant of all. Greatness comes in one's service to others.

> "For who separates you from the others [as a faction leader]? [Who makes you superior and sets you apart from another, giving you the preeminence?] What have you that was not given to you? If then you received it [from someone], why do you boast as if you had not received [but had gained it by your own efforts]?"(1 Corinthians 4:7 AMP)

There would be no need to brag or promote oneself if believers understood that all they have, and all they are, is because of Christ. He is the giver of life and the giver of every good and perfect gift. It is okay to boast in the Lord, as David did in the face of Goliath, but it is never right to posses a superior attitude towards others.

> "For I say, through the grace given unto me, to every man that is among you, not to think of himself more highly than he ought to think; but to think soberly, according as God hath dealt to every man the measure of faith. Having then gifts differing according to the grace that is given to us, whether prophecy, let us prophesy according to the proportion of faith." (Romans 12:3, 6 KJV)

Choose to think of yourself soberly in light of God's grace and mercy. In all of your endeavors, don't compare your work to another's, but focus on pleasing God and succeeding in the eyes of Him to whom we give account. Love seeks to give all glory to God and reflects the spirit of meekness in all of life. This causes others to see the root of ones success and directs the glory and honor and praise to God.

## LOVE IS NOT PRIDEFUL

Love is not inflated with pride. The love of God has within it no form of arrogance or smugness. From the beginning of time, pride has been a downfall, a perfect example of which was found in Lucifer. His fall from heaven was a direct result of the pride that was rooted in his heart. Pride always has its root in self "…lest being lifted up with pride he fall into the condemnation of the devil" (I Tim 3:6 KJV). It is important not to have an exaggerated view of one's own importance. This is possible as we see ourselves fully in the light of God's grace. As new creations in Christ Jesus, believers are still nothing apart from Him. He is the inexhaustible source of whom they have great need. It pays to live humbly before God, acknowledging Him in every way. It is then the church will be able to see people as He sees, and to look upon others without class distinctions and disparagements.

> "Nay, much more those members of the body, which seem to be more feeble, are necessary: And those members of the body, which we think to be less honorable, upon these we bestow more abundant honor; and our uncomely parts have more abundant comeliness. For our comely parts have no need: but God hath tempered the body together, having given more abundant honor to that part which lacked: That there should be no schism in the body; but that the members should have the same care one for another. And whether one member suffers, all the members suffer with it; or one member be honored, all the members rejoice with it." (I Corinthians 12:22- 26 KJV)

Christians are called to love in this manner, to treat others as Christ has treated them. God hates a prideful spirit because it is an attitude that enthrones itself in the place of God. It chooses self-government, self-reliance and self-success over the rule of God. Belshazzar's is an example of this, *"And thou his son, O Belshazzar, hast not humbled thine heart ... but hast lifted up thyself against the Lord of heaven."(Dan 5: 22 -23 KJV)* This man made a huge mistake by not glorifying God with his accomplishments.

> *But he giveth more grace. Wherefore he saith, God resisteth the proud, but giveth grace unto the humble."*
> *(James 4:6 KJV)*

The reason God gives grace to the humble is because they glorify Him, and as He extends more grace, they glorify Him even more. The greater the accomplishment, the greater is He glorified in the eyes of man. This is why He continues to pour out more and more grace to those who are humble. It is the proud that He resists, or sets Himself against. The church must make every effort to be clothed with the humility of Christ and allow Him to be glorified through their lives.

## LOVE IS NOT RUDE

Love does not behave in an ugly, indecent and unseemly manner. It avoids disgracing, mistreating or dishonoring someone with the intent of causing harm. Rude people act in defiance of social and moral standards, which results in disgrace, embarrassment, and shame. Love behaves in a manner that believes the best in people. It is approachable and easy to be entreated. God's love is full of kindness and tenderness and believers must take on and exemplify this same love.

> *"Put on therefore, as the elect of God, holy and beloved, bowels of mercies, kindness, humbleness of mind, meekness, longsuffering." (Colossians 3:12 KJV)*

## LOVE IS NOT SELF SEEKING

*"For all seek their own, not the things which are Jesus Christ's."(Phil 2:21 KJV)* The least kind of life a person can live is a life centered on self. Christ is the perfect example of one who lived a self-less life (1 John 4:9-10). He gave of Himself, even to the death of the cross, on behalf of humanity. If a person hasn't lived for Christ, then in all actuality, they haven't really lived (Phil 1: 21). It is making Him the focus and center of ones life that brings true satisfaction. Life is more than making a living; believers are not called to preserve their own lives, but to live for Christ and for the cause of the kingdom. *"Seek ye first the Kingdom of God."* This is the priority of a Christian's life. To

seek the kingdom means to seek the character of Christ and the principles of His Kingdom. It means to use all that one had and all that they are to fulfill His cause in the earth. Christians were created to serve God by serving the ones he died for. *"Look not every man on his own things, but every man also on things of others" (Phil 2:4 KJV).* God's love is a love that lays down its life for the good of others (I John 4:11). So living a selfless life is part of walking and growing in the love of God.

> *"Then Peter began to say unto him, Lo, we have left all, and have followed thee. And Jesus answered and said, Verily I say unto you, There is no man that hath left house, or brethren, or sisters, or father, or mother, or wife, or children, or lands, for my sake, and the gospel's, But he shall receive an hundredfold now in this time, houses, and brethren, and sisters, and mothers, and children, and lands, with persecutions; and in the world to come eternal life." (Mark 10:28-30 KJV)*

## LOVE IS NOT EASILY PROVOKED

Love is not fretful, resentful, or touchy. It doesn't get easily upset and it is not contentious. It is neither irritable nor is it moody. If these attitudes are prevalent in a person, it points to something deeper. It is a clear sign that a person's emotions are out of control due to the passivity of the inner-man.

> *"If thou faint in the day of adversity, thy strength is small." (Proverbs 24:10 KJV)*

When a believer is passive in spiritual things, he is open to all sorts of attacks from the evil one. Little things can easily escalate and be blown out of proportion. This is why God's word encourages believers to be strong in the Lord (Eph 6:10). When a person loses control in the inner-man, they also lose control of both soul and body (I Corinthians 9:27).

*"He that hath no rule over his own spirit is like a city that is broken down, and without walls" (Pr 25:28 KJV)*. Passivity is the loss of exercising the will in controlling the spirit, soul and body (I Corinthians 7:37). When the inner-man is not being exercised, it remains passive, and can easily be poisoned by the fiery darts of the wicked one. In order to live from a place of victory, ones spirit-man must develop strength. This is how a person becomes strong in spirit (Luke 1:80).

It is imperative that Christians learn to walk after the Spirit (Gal 5:25), mind the Spirit (Rom 8:5), and put spiritual things first. This should not sound strange; it is the normal function of a healthy spirit. When a person's spirit is healthy, it is proved by the full operation of the fruit of the spirit (Gal 5:22), just like fruit is indicative of a healthy tree. Love reveals itself in self-control, a heart that is free from all anxiety, fear, agitation and anything else that is able to contaminate the Spirit life.

## LOVE THINKS NO EVIL

Love keeps no record of wrongdoing. This is a powerful virtue in the character of Christ; He keeps no record of people's faults and failures. He doesn't even hold a sinner's sin against him. *"...Not imputing their trespasses unto them (II Corinthians 5:19)*. It's cancerous to keep negative, bitter memories in ones mind. It affects the entire nervous system and poisons billions of cells. It is important to be deliberate about not setting ones mind on evil and keeping no record of wrongdoing.

How would you feel, if God remembered all your faults and chose to keep them active in His memory? What if He chose to never to forgive and forget? And how would you feel, if he constantly reminded you of all your shortcomings?

> *"For I will be merciful to their unrighteousness, and their sins and their iniquities will I remember no more."*
> *(Hebrews 8:12 KJV)*

> *"I, even I, am he that blotteth out thy transgressions for mine own sake, and will not remember thy sins." (Isaiah 43:25 KJV)*

It is possible to forgive and forget wrongs committed by others. Remember, everyone has fallen short and done hurtful things, yet God chooses to keep no record of it. People have done things to the Father's heart that are far worse than what others have done to them. So take on the character of Christ in practice (Gal 3:27). God's Word tells believers what to set their minds upon (Phil 4:8), and as they meditate and practice these scriptures, they will naturally take on Christ.

## LOVE REJOICES IN THE TRUTH

> *"And in thy majesty ride prosperously because of truth…" (Psalms 45:4 KJV)*

Truth is the cornerstone of the kingdom of God. This is why Satan attempts to veil people from it. Hiding the light of truth is the only way to keep the world in darkness and eternal perdition. The enemy must sell lies in order to deceive the human race. *"And that the whole world is under the control of the evil one." (1 John 5:19 GWT)* Once a person believes the lies of Satan, his mind plunges into darkness and is veiled from the truth. Without knowing it, he becomes a captive of Satan (II Tim 2: 25-26). The deceptions of the enemy only thrive on a platform of lies, and these lies become strongholds when they become a part of one's belief systems. Satan, the prince of darkness, is fundamentally a liar by nature.

> *You are of your father, the devil, and it is your will to practice the lusts and gratify the desires [which are characteristic] of your father. He was a murderer from the beginning and does not stand in the truth, because there is no truth in him. When he speaks a falsehood, he speaks what is natural to him, for he is a liar [himself]*

> *and the father of lies and of all that is false." (John 8:44 AMP)*

Satan is a real enemy and should not be taken lightly. He is a liar, a deceiver, a murderer and he hates the Lord Jesus Christ. He is out to destroy all things beautiful, and does so by selling his lies or sometimes, incomplete truth. *"Now the Spirit speaketh expressly, that in the latter times some shall depart from the faith, giving heed to seducing spirits, and doctrines of devils" (I Tim 4:1 KJV)*. Take the issue of abortion. The only way a nation could murder 50 million innocent babies is by believing a lie. This lie has caused more death than WWI and WWII combined. Now is the time for the church body to rise up and stand on the pillar of truth.

## THE TRIUMPH OF TRUTH

The way to contend with Satan's lies is to engage him with the weapon of truth. *"Sanctify them through thy truth; thy word is truth" (John 17:17 KJV)*. Truth has one origin just as lies have one origin; truth comes from Jesus Christ. *"Jesus said unto him, I am the way, the truth, and the life: no man cometh unto the Father, but by me." (John 14:6 KJV)* His truth is displayed in His life and His message. God's Word is His truth, and it must be spread throughout the world, in the power of God's Spirit. The Spirit of truth only works where Christ's truth prevails. He is in the earth to give witness of Christ's death, burial and resurrection. He is to bear witness to His sacrifice, His blood, His work and His deity.

> *"FURTHERMORE, BRETHREN, do pray for us, that the Word of the Lord may speed on (spread rapidly and run its course) and be glorified (extolled) and triumph, even as [it has done] with you." (II Thessalonians 3:1 AMP)*

It is time for the church to become humble and to become a house of prayer (Isa 56:9). One who labors in prayer through the power of the Spirit, and uses the sword of the Spirit (Eph 6:17) against the lies of Satan (II Co 1:3-6) will cause truth to triumph. To put on God's love, Christians must embrace His truth as their own. It is the only defense against Satan's lies. There is no other way to give truth to a lost and dying world unless people are possessors of truth. It must prevail and dominate their hearts and lives. The entire character and conduct of Christians must be built and established on the cornerstone of truth. As they live in this manner, they will prevail and win the world back to Jesus Christ by influencing their systems with His truth. It will expose the Spirit of error and lift the veil of deception from those bound by its influence.

## LOVE IS THE KING'S CHARACTER

In these last days, the church must clothe herself with the character of the King of the Kingdom (Gal 3:24), if she is to be relevant and full of power. Nothing can make the church more beautiful than taking on in practice the character of Christ. God's expectation for every believer is to grow into the measure of the stature of the fullness of Christ. This is to become their lifestyle. There is no counterfeit for the character of God, which is love. Love is not a feeling, but rather a habit that is cultivated through practice. The world must see Him as He is, and as the church becomes like Him, they will see Him through His church and be transformed by His presence.

## HOW LOVE TRANSFORMED AN UNGODLY ENTERPRISE

A young man from Indonesia had inherited multiple businesses from his late father, and among these were a 5 Star hotel and a motel. The motel, however, was simply a prostitute joint. It was home to well over two thousand prostitution-related activities a week. The young man, unlike his father, was a committed Christian and he had a desire to transform the motel into a business built and established on Christian values and Christian principles. After seeking for God's wisdom, he decided to hire some pastors who would come to the motel on a daily bases, not to preach but only to pray. They set up a prayer altar in the motel and started praying for a total overhaul of the business.

For weeks upon weeks, they prayed for these precious souls. After a while, they strategically planned to meet the needs of both the prostitutes and their clients by offering to pray for their needs. Even at this point, the gospel message was not being preached. The prostitutes started coming in for prayer and had their hearts transformed in remarkable ways. They were moved by the love of these pastors, who were also serving as host and hostesses. After doing this for 2 years, all the prostitutes were transformed and as a result, most of their clients were as well. They knew they could no longer continue in their old practices and, therefore, chose to give it up. They were offered training in order to help them acquire skills for credible employment. Not only were their souls saved, but the motel was completely transformed into a business that honored God by uprooting worldly value-systems and replacing them with the value-system of God.

This principle may sound very simple, but it always works. If a person really has a heart to reach out and make a difference in peoples lives, follow these guidelines: 1) love the lost, 2) build relationships, 3) meet a need and 4) present the gospel. These simple principles are very basic, but they bring profound results.

# Chapter 6
# THE ESSENCE OF THE SALT LIFE
## "KINGDOM KEYS TO THE DISCIPLESHIP OF NATIONS"

Salt is used for its ability to bring change. It contains the power to make something that is unappealing become full of flavor. Saltiness flavors food by suppressing other taste responses such as sweet, sour, and bitter. Its value, therefore, is in its power and not in its color. When salt loses its power to effect change, it loses its value and becomes worthless. In the same way, the church loses her value when she lacks transformational ability. The essence of the salt life, therefore, is found in its power to transform nations. The transformation of nations is the primary assignment of the Church as well as the fundamental requirement of the Great Commission given by the Lord Jesus Himself.

### THE GREAT COMMISSION DEFINED

> *"All authority (all power of rule) in heaven and on earth has been given to Me. Go then and make disciples of all the nations, baptizing them into the name of the Father and of the Son and of the Holy Spirit, Teaching them to observe everything that I have commanded you, and behold, I am with you all the days...to the very close and consummation of the age. Amen." (Matthew 28:18-20 AMP)*

Most Christians have been taught a one-dimensional view of the Great Commission. Even in my own life I had difficulty understanding it as an adolescent growing up in Africa. The reason is that the Great Commission was taught solely in the context of soul winning and evangelism. At the early age of 12, I was the evangelism coordinator for the Scripture Union organization in my village. This organization was deeply rooted in the belief that the Great Commission meant going from house to house, knocking on doors, giving tracts, and telling the good-news. I was also taught that this mandate included holding open-air crusades with the sole intent of bringing people to the saving knowledge of Jesus Christ. Because this concept was wrong, it limited my effectiveness, yet I grew, and so did my understanding. It was several years ago that a new understanding of the Great Commission took hold of my heart. It is more than soul winning or evangelism. It is more than open-air crusades. There is so much more substance to this mandate.

To understand the discipling of nations it must be properly defined. This will help lift the veil and cause the body of Christ to see the truth. It is paramount that the church understands the intent of Jesus' statement so she can accomplish it accordingly. The Great Commission, according to Matthew 28:18-20, includes two main characteristics 1) The Discipleship of Nations and 2) The Baptism of Nations. It is the call to transform the systems and structures of this world with the character of the King and the values of His Kingdom.

## THE DISCIPLESHIP OF NATIONS

The discipleship of Nations not only deals with the salvation of a person's soul, it also includes the transformation of ones environment. Nations like Guatemala, Romania, Armenia, and Nigeria strongly validate this point. These nations have as many as 90-95% of their population professing Christianity. Some have even had Christian presidents, heads of state, senators and other top members of parliament. Yet, systemic corruption and poverty exists so rampantly in these nations. The social, political, educational and economic structures are some of the weakest in the world and as a result, citizens are suffering at an alarming rate. In many parts of Africa there are very vibrant churches. Nigeria, for example, has a reputation for pulling in the largest crowds in evangelistic campaigns, some even numbering in the millions for single, one-night events. It is a great achievement for any country to cross such thresholds in the history of Christianity, but the gospel is meant to transform not only mankind, but also the very structures upon which nations are built.

Take for example, a man who has lived under a bridge for 25 years in a community infested with drugs, prostitution and crime. For someone like this to come to Christ is a tremendous victory, but if he is returned to the same environment it will be but a temporal change. The gospel must transform not only him, but his environment as well. The gospel is designed to affect both the person and the society where he or she lives. As previously stated in this book, the Great Commission addresses structures and value-systems of any given society. This is what Jesus meant when He gave the mandate to disciple the nations of the world. It is displacing the values of this world and replacing them with the values of the Kingdom of God. Every nation is built on seven structures and these structures must be built and established on kingdom values in order to have sustenance and lasting prosperity.

## THE BAPTISM OF NATIONS

When Jesus said to baptize them into the name of the Father, Son and Holy Spirit, it means to immerse the values of this world into a three-fold baptism. It is a baptism into the life, nature and character of the Godhead. Nations are to be fully immersed through this baptism until all of its structures, systems, values and culture are transformed. The government of Christ must permeate and dominate the kingdoms of this world. Every fiber of a nation's life and operation must be seen reflecting from within it the very values of Christ. Just as the taking on of Christ's nature and character reflects Christ in every way, so must nations take on the values of the kingdom to reflect God's rule in every way. The values and virtues of Christ are to be stamped into the very DNA of every nation until it becomes the culture and standard of that nation (Gal 3:27).

## THE POWER OF THE SALTED LIFE

Salt is only as useful as its ability to bring about change. Its relevance lies solely in its power to transform. The outward color, as beautiful as it looks, is of no value without its functional abilities. The church, as the body of Christ, should measure true evangelical success not only by the number of people who commit their lives to Christ, but also by the wealth of the values and virtues of the kingdom that are represented in their communities, cities, state and nation. The Great Commission requires the transformation of every nation into a kingdom culture and a baptism of its values into the character of Christ. The relevance of the New Testament church is in her ability to transform nations. She is to be known for her works and not her religious clichés. *"If I do not the works of my Father, believe me not." (John 10:37 KJV)* Every Christian needs a fresh understanding of the Great Commission. The ability to effectively reach the world for Christ lies within this understanding. Remember that wisdom is better than strength and wisdom is better than weapons of war (Eccl 9:16, 18). Often, the church has little measurement of success as it relates to the Great Commission and this ignorance has cost her wasted efforts, energy, time, and resources. Furthermore, it will take humility, a teachable spirit and a willingness to adjust ones mindset and shift the old concept of the Great Commission to a more complete view of this heavenly mandate.

## THE POWER TO CHANGE THE WORLD

*"Ask of me, and I shall give thee the heathen for thine inheritance, and the uttermost parts of the earth for thy possession." (Psalms 2:8 KJV)*

God has literally given His church the power needed to change the world. In the Great Commission, Jesus said that all authority has been given to Him and to go into the world and make disciples of all the nations. Christians are to go forth with the authority of Jesus, which is His royal and legal right to rule the world. Through His death and resurrection, He conquered Satan, hell and death. He paid the price for the salvation of man and for the redemption of creation. In the fall, Adam lost both himself and his God-given authority over the earth, but Jesus, in the Great Commission, restored that authority back to the church. Believers are now the managers of the earth and have a responsibility to exercise dominion, meaning the right to rule and the power to execute God's justice and righteousness throughout the earth. God has given to every child the right and power to reign in any and all spheres of life.

## KINGDOM KEYS TO TRANSFORMING THE WORLD

*"And Jesus went about all the cities and villages, teaching in their synagogues, and preaching the gospel of the kingdom, and healing every sickness and every disease among the people. But when he saw the multitudes, he was moved with compassion on them, because they fainted, and were scattered abroad, as sheep having no shepherd. Then saith he unto his disciples, The harvest truly is plenteous, but the laborers are few; Pray ye therefore the Lord of the harvest, that he will send forth laborers into his harvest." (Matthew 9:35-38 KJV)*

*"Say not ye, There are yet four months, and then cometh the harvest? Behold, I say unto you, Lift up your eyes, and look on the fields; for they are white already to harvest." (John 4:35 KJV)* Until a person puts on the eyes of God, they cannot see as He sees. God gave His children the ability to see the true condition of the world. Every believer, every church, must lift up their eyes beyond self and see the multitudes, see the widow, the fatherless, and millions of orphans with shattered dreams. See the sick and afflicted and millions who won't live to see another year. They must see the world, the Muslim world, the Hindu world, the New-Age world, the Buddhist world, and the Arab world. The eyes of the church must be opened. The world is destitute when millions are living in bondage to the power of sin. Take a look at the depth of systemic corruption and poverty, injustice and lawlessness in the world. If people could see as He

sees, they would understand the true value of a soul. They are God's only treasure and they are priceless. It took God's very own Son to pay for them. Listed below are the keys needed for every believer to be an agent of change.

- The heart must be moved: *"Now while Paul waited for them at Athens, his spirit was stirred in him, when he saw the city wholly given to idolatry" (Acts 17:16 KJV).* Something moved in the heart of Paul when he saw the godless condition of the land. Likewise, the believer's heart must be moved at the condition of humanity today and their value-system. It is important for believers's to guard themselves against hardness of heart and to become sensitive to the needs of others. *"For I have no man likeminded, who will naturally care for your state. For all seek their own, not the things which are Jesus Christ's" (Phil 2:20-21 KJV).* The Christian life can be summarized as loving God and loving people. The truth is that the church needs a heart transplant; she needs to receive the heart that Jesus had for people. It was a love so strong that He offered His very life for it. This is what living is truly all about and those who have experienced it understand the joy and power that comes from a Christ-centered life. For a person's heart to move, their eyes must be able to see. *Pray that God would open your eyes to see the true condition of what is going on all around you.*

- Be moved with compassion: Compassion is more than feeling sorry for someone or having pity for someone. Compassion is always accompanied by action. The actions of compassion go beyond providing temporary relief; it strives to deal with root causes. It contains a strong desire to make life-changing differences in one's life. It is easy to measure the difference that can be made in a person's life by the amount of money one has, but what is even more important is the size of one's heart and the size of his or her faith. The Bible is full of people who changed the world through their faith in God. A good place to start is to take on the burdens of others in prayer. As a strong and disciplined prayer life is cultivated, the Holy Spirit will deposit His emotions for the lost in ones heart. They will able to feel what He feels and sees what He sees. The Holy Spirit will teach a person how to co-labor with Christ, the great Intercessor, over the condition of humanity and creation as a whole. Christians will discover a new power in prayer and will accomplish great things as they gain new levels of authority in the spirit. Furthermore, this prayer will compel one to action. Remember that true compassion must transcend mere emotion of the soul. It has to be imparted by the Holy Spirit, into the human spirit, with tangible deeds that transform.

- Understand the gospel of the kingdom: *"And Jesus went about all the cities and villages, teaching in their synagogues, and preaching the gospel of the kingdom, and healing every sickness and every disease among the people"* (Matt 9:35 KJV). The gospel of the kingdom involves the healing of all sickness and disease. It is easy to think only in terms of bodily ailments such as cancer, diabetes, etc. However, it also includes political and educational diseases, social and economic diseases, systemic corruption and systemic poverty. It includes all human and societal ills, everything affecting people and society at large. In-fact, all social diseases either directly or indirectly affecting mankind needs the healing touch of Jesus. This is why Jesus went to different villages and cities, preaching the gospel of the kingdom. He didn't choose which sicknesses to heal; He healed all manner of diseases among the people. By healing the sick, Jesus destroyed and displaced the works of darkness that came upon humanity as a result of the fall (Rom 5:12). So the gospel of the kingdom enthrones the rule of Christ in man and in society. Just as the lordship of Christ should have full sway in man's spirit, soul and body, so also should the government of God have full sway in every sphere of society.

- Pray to the Lord of the harvest: *"Pray ye therefore the Lord of the harvest, that he will send forth laborers into his harvest" (Matt 9:38 KJV)*. This statement, when understood, contains a very powerful truth that will shake the kingdom of darkness at its core. The word "Lord" actually means "Owner." As believer's pray for the lost, they must pray with the understanding the Jesus is the Lord of the harvest. He is the owner of the harvest. Why? He paid for the salvation of man and for the redemption of creation. Remember, He bought the field and the field is the world. He bought the field and the treasure in the field (Matt 13:44, 38). The field represents the cosmos and the structures upon which a nation is built, while the treasure represents the people who live in the world. The blood of Christ is the price that was paid and the ground on which creation shall be delivered into the liberty of the sons of God (Rom 8:21). The same price that paid for the soul of man paid for his environment; therefore God places equal emphasis on both. The former governs the latter. So Christians should pray with a fresh revelation that because of the blood of Christ, all souls potentially belong to Christ. He died for all, and therefore, all should live for Him (2 Co. 5:14-15). Imagine knowing that the forces of darkness no longer determine the harvesting of souls, although people may be under their spell (1John 5:19). Imagine knowing that God determines the harvest of souls based on the prayer and the labor of the saints. The prayer is for laborers to be sent out into the harvest field, while the laborers work and reap the harvest. It is a labor in a field that belongs to Christ. Begin to see the unsaved in God's harvest field and not in the hand of Satan. Ask the owner of the harvest to give you the harvest. They belong to Him because the price has been paid.

**KINGDOM KEYS TO THE DISCIPESHIP OF NATIONS**

- Understand that every nation is built on seven structures

- Understand that to transform a nation, every structure must be transformed
- Understand that the local church is to raise saviors to bring change
- Individuals must pursue Christ-likeness
- They must discover their specific assignment
- It must translate into a specific area of influence
- This influence must be a platform to bring the Kingdom of God
- This area of influence must be related to one of the seven structures of the nation
- Their assignment must address and transform a specific societal ill
- They must understand the specific structure they want to change
- They must access the wisdom of God for the specific blueprint on how to bring about transformation
- They must find a like-minded team to work together
- They must work hard at executing the plan
- They must set up kingdom structures and value systems to sustain godliness and lasting prosperity
- They must set up ancient landmarks for the next generation

# CONCLUSION

Although this book is filled with a lot of information, its value is determined in how much of it is put into practice. It will take reading, studying and meditating on the principles in this book to form a mindset that views Christianity through the discipleship of nations. Christians must believe that transformation is possible and that there is enough greatness in one person to make a significant difference. The Bible says in Psalm 115:16 *"The heaven, even the heavens, are the Lord's: but the earth hath he given to the children of men."* God is managing the affairs of heaven because that is His territory, His domain. Even though His influence extends to the earth, the responsibility to manage it has been given to the children of men. The earth is to be managed by its inhabitants and the Holy Spirit will help them to pattern it after the blueprint of heaven.

> *"Thy kingdom come, Thy will be done in earth, as it is in heaven." (Matthew 6:10 KJV)*

No one should look around and ask, "Where is God?" God has chosen to reign in the earth through His church. This is His design and His plan, and the reason why the body of Christ must reflect the same Jesus who walked the earth 2000 years ago. The only people who should be asking the whereabouts of God are those in the world, and the answer should be found shining forth from the church.

> *"Out of Zion, the perfection of beauty, God hath shined." (Psalms 50:1-2 KJV)*

The church is the light of the world and the salt of the earth. She is a city set on a hill for all to see. The church is the mountain that is established above all mountains, a shining light to the nations of the world. When the church becomes the beacon of light she was designed to be; it will prepare the way for the fulfillment of the Great Commission. It is from this position of strength that people can be effectively trained and released into the world to engage the culture and bring in the values and character of Christ.

Made in the USA
San Bernardino, CA
28 December 2018